The Ninja Foodi Pressure Cooker Cookbook

1000 Healthy, Easy and Delicious Recipes to Pressure Cook, Slow Cook, Air Fry, Dehydrate, and much more.

Keven Abernathy

© Copyright 2020 -All rights reserved.

Disclaimer Notice:

Please note the information contained within this document is for educational and entertainment purposes only. Every attempt has been made to provide accurate, up to date and reliable, complete information. No warranties of any kind are expressed or implied. Readers acknowledge that the author is not engaging in the rendering of legal, financial, medical or professional advice. By reading this document, the reader agrees that under no circumstances are we responsible for any losses, direct or indirect, which are incurred as a result of the use of information contained within this document, including, but not limited to, errors, omissions, or inaccuracies.

Legal Notice:

This book is copyright protected. This is only for personal use. You cannot amend, distribute, sell, use, quote or paraphrase any part or the content within this book without the consent of the author or copyright owner. Legal action will be pursued if this is breached.

The information provided herein is stated to be truthful and consistent, in that any liability, regarding inattention or otherwise, by any usage or abuse of any policies, processes, or directions contained within is the solitary and complete responsibility of the recipient reader. Under no circumstances will any legal liability or blame be held against the publisher for any reparation, damages, or monetary loss due to the information herein, either directly or indirectly. Respective authors own all copyrights not held by the publisher.

The author is not a licensed practitioner, physician or medical professional and offers no medical treatment, diagnoses, suggestions or counselling. The information presented herein has not been evaluated by the US Food & Drug Administration, and it is not intended to diagnose, treat, cure or prevent any disease. Full medical clearance from a licensed physician should be obtained before beginning or modifying any diet, exercise or lifestyle program, and physician should be informed of all nutritional changes. The author claims no responsibility to any person or entity for any liability, loss, damage or death caused or alleged to be caused directly or indirectly as a result of the use, application or interpretation of the information presented herein.

Table of Contents

Table of Contents 5

Introduction 13

Chapter 1: Why Ninja Foodi? 15

Ninja Foodi is Your Only Kitchen Gadget 15

Ninja Foodi Combines Pressure Cooker with Air Fryer 15

It Works Automatically 16

It Helps Plan Meals Ahead of Time 16

365 Meals- All-in-One Pot Meals 16

It is Quick and Time-Saving 17

It Uses Less Oil 18

It Saves Energy 18

It Makes Dishes Tender Inside and Crispy Outside 18

It can Cook Frozen Ingredients 19

The Food Will be Nutritional and Delicious 19

Other Benefits of Ninja Foodi Cooking 19

Why is it Better Than Instant Pot, Slow Cooker or Air Fryer? 20

Chapter 2: Ninja Foodi 101 21

Different Models of Ninja Foodi 21

Review the Magic of Ninja Foodi One-by-one 21

Operating Buttons: 22

Steps of Using Ninja Foodi 22

Essential Tips and Tricks for Newbies 23

Additional tips to make the most of the cooking functions: 24

Cautions You Must Know 24

Ninja Foodi Trouble Shooting 25

PRESSURE COOKING GUIDE 26

AIR CRISPING COOKING GUIDE (Using the Cook & Crisp Basket) 28

STEAMING GUIDE (Using the Reversible Rack) 29
FAQs..29

Chapter 3: Ninja Foodi Shopping and Maintenance........................33

Where to Shop for it 33
How to Choose Your Suitable Ninja Foodi...34
How to Maintain it...34

Chapter 4: Ninja Foodi Pressure Cooker Recipes 37
Breakfast Recipes 37

1. Breakfast Frittata 37
2. Egg in Toast 38
3. Baked Eggs...38
4. Breakfast Potatoes 39
5. Egg & Turkey Sausage Cups 40
6. Omelette...41
7. Cheesy Broccoli Quiche 42
8. Bacon & Scrambled Eggs 43
9. French Toast 43
10. Eggs & Veggie Burrito..44
11. Breakfast Casserole 45
12. Herb & Cheese Frittata 46
13. Roasted Garlic Potatoes 47
14. Tofu Scramble 48
15. Avocado Egg 49
16. Butter Melted Broccoli Florets...49
17. The Epic Fried Eggs...50
18. Gentle Keto Butter Fish 50
19. Sensational Carrot Puree 51
20. Simple Broccoli Florets 52
21. Awesome Magical 5 Ingredient Shrimp 52

22. Romantic Mustard Pork ... 53
23. Creative And Easy Lamb Roast ... 53
24. Crispy Tofu And Mushrooms ... 54
25. A Hearty Sausage Meal ... 55
26. Deserving Mushroom Saute ... 55
27. Slightly Zesty Lamb Chops ... 56
28. Bacon And Scrambled Egg ... 56
29. Delicious Creamy Crepes ... 57
30. Egg Stuffed Avocado Dish ... 58

Beef, Pork and Lamb Recipes ... 59

1. Beef Stir Fry ... 59
2. Mongolian Beef ... 60
3. Beef & Broccoli ... 61
4. Beef Stew ... 62
5. Asian Beef ... 63
6. Pork Chops in Honey Mustard Sauce ... 64
7. Crispy Pork Chops ... 65
8. Garlic Butter Pork ... 66
9. Pork with Gravy ... 67
10. Hawaiian Pork ... 68
11. Middle Eastern Lamb Stew ... 69
12. Lamb Curry ... 70
13. Mediterranean Lamb Roast ... 71
14. Braised Lamb Shanks ... 72
15. Rosemary Lamb Chops ... 73
16. Tantalizing Beef Jerky ... 74
17. Beefed Up Spaghetti Squash ... 75
18. Adobo Cubed Steak ... 75
19. Cool Beef Bourguignon ... 76
20. A Keto-Friendly Philly Willy Steak And Cheese ... 77

21. Beef Stew 78
22. Juiciest Keto Bacon Strips 78
23. Quick Picadillo Dish 79
24. Simple/Aromatic Meatballs 80
25. Generous Shepherd's Pie 80
26. Hybrid Beef Prime Roast 81
27. The Epic Carne Guisada 82
28. No-Noodle Pure Lasagna 82
29. The Wisdom Worthy Corned Beef 83
30. Hearty Korean Ribs 84
31. Traditional Beef Sirloin Steak 85
32. Beef And Broccoli Platter 85
33. Alternative Corned Cabbage And Beef 87

Chicken and Poultry Recipes 89

1. Crispy Roast Chicken 89
2. Ranch Chicken Wings 90
3. Chicken Parmesan 91
4. Honey Chicken Wings 91
5. Chicken Nuggets 92
6. Peanut Chicken 93
7. Honey Teriyaki Chicken 94
8. Turkey & Broccoli 95
9. Garlic Paprika Turkey Thighs 96
10. Chicken Carnitas 97
11. Lemon Chicken with Garlic 98
12. Chicken Cacciatore 99
13. Chicken Marsala 100
14. Barbecue Chicken 102
15. Chicken Chile Verde 102
16. Lemon And Chicken Extravaganza 103

17. Bruschetta Chicken Meal 104
18. The Great Hainanese Chicken 105
19. A Genuine Hassel Back Chicken 106
20. Shredded Up Salsa Chicken 106
21. Mexico's Favorite Chicken Soup 107
22. Taiwanese Chicken Delight 107
23. Cabbage And Chicken Meatballs 108
24. Poached Chicken With Coconut Lime Cream Sauce 109
25. Hot And Spicy Paprika Chicken 110
26. Inspiring Turkey Cutlets 110
27. Lemongrass And Tamarind Chicken 111
28. Fluffy Whole Chicken Dish 112
29. Sensible Chettinad Chicken 112
30. Hawaiian Pinna Colada Chicken Meal 114
31. Garlic and Butter Chicken Dish 114
32. Creamy Chicken Curry 115
33. Lemon And Artichoke Medley 115
34. Awesome Sesame Ginger Chicken 116
35. Chicken Korma 117
36. Turkey With Garlic Sauce 118

Fish and Seafood Recipes 119

1. Fish & Fries 119
2. Ranch Fish Fillet 120
3. Paprika Salmon 121
4. Fish & Chips with Herb Sauce 121
5. Southern Fried Fish Fillet 123
6. Fish Sticks 124
7. Fish Fillet with Pesto Sauce 125
8. Coconut Shrimp 126
9. Hot Prawns 127

10. Crispy Shrimp 127
11. Salt and Pepper Shrimp 128
12. Tuna Patties 129
13. Lemon Garlic Shrimp 130
14. Crispy Cod Fish 131
15. Crispy Fish Nuggets 132
16. Heartfelt Sesame Fish 132
17. Awesome Sock-Eye Salmon 133
18. Buttered Up Scallops 134
19. Awesome Cherry Tomato Mackerel 134
20. Lovely Air Fried Scallops 135
21. Packets Of Lemon And Dill Cod 135
22. Adventurous Sweet And Sour Fish 136
23. Garlic And Lemon Prawn Delight 137
24. Lovely Carb Soup 137
25. The Rich Guy Lobster And Butter 138
26. Lovely Panko Cod 139
27. Salmon Paprika 139
28. Heartfelt Air Fried Scampi 140
29. Ranch Warm Fillets 141
30. Alaskan Cod Divine 141
31. Kale And Salmon Delight 142
32. Breathtaking Cod Fillets 143
33. Lemon And Pepper Salmon Delight 144
34. Fresh Steamed Salmon 145

Vegan and Vegetarian Recipes 147

1. Fried Soy Curls 147
2. Crispy Tofu 148
3. Onion Rings 148
4. Potato Wedges 149

5. Buffalo Cauliflower 150
6. Garlic Chips 151
7. Cauliflower Stir Fry 152
8. Vegan Cheese Sticks 153
9. Smoked Chickpeas 154
10. Fried Broccoli 154
11. Tofu, Broccoli and Carrot 155
12. Fried Tempeh 156
13. Garlic Pepper Potato Chips 157
14. Brussels Sprouts 158
15. Vegetable Fritters 159
16. Crazy Fresh Onion Soup 160
17. Elegant Zero Crust Kale And Mushroom Quiche 160
18. Delicious Beet Borscht 161
19. Pepper Jack Cauliflower Meal 162
20. Slow-Cooked Brussels 163
21. Slowly Cooked Lemon Artichokes 163
22. Well Dressed Brussels 164
23. Cheddar Cauliflower Bowl 164
24. A Prosciutto And Thyme Eggs 165
25. The Authentic Zucchini Pesto Meal 166
26. Supreme Cauliflower Soup 167
27. Very Rich And Creamy Asparagus Soup 168
28. Summertime Vegetable Platter 168
29. The Creative Mushroom Stroganoff 169
30. Garlic And Ginger Red Cabbage Platter 170
31. The Veggie Lover's Onion And Tofu Platter 170
32. Feisty Maple Dredged Carrots 171
33. The Original Sicilian Cauliflower Roast 172

Grains and Beans 175

1. Fried Green Beans 175
2. Navy Beans with Ham 175
3. Roasted Chickpeas 176
4. Spicy Green Beans 177
5. Baked Beans 178
6. Sausage & Beans 179
7. Tomato & Beans 180
8. Lemon Butter Green Beans 181

Soups and Stews 183

1. Beef & Potato Stew 183
2. Potato Soup 184
3. Cauliflower Soup 185
4. Beef & Vegetable Soup 186
5. Ham & Potato Soup 187
6. Minestrone Soup 188
7. Tomato Basil Soup 190
8. Chicken & Lemon Soup 191

Side Dishes 193

1. Garlic Mushrooms 193
2. Mediterranean Vegetables 194
3. Fried Carrots, Zucchini and Squash 195
4. Honey Roasted Carrots 196
5. Roasted Corn 196
6. Sweet Potato 197
7. Lemon Parmesan Broccoli 198
8. Garlic Mashed Potatoes 199

Conclusion 201

Appendix 1: Measurement Conversion Table 203

Appendix 2: Common Healthy Food for Living 205

Introduction

The increasing demand for healthy, quick, and delicious meals has given rise to all sorts of kitchen gadgets that are meant to transform anyone into a kitchen god/goddess.

One such appliance is the Ninja Foodi, a gadget that combines pressure-cooking and air-frying in one nifty unit.

This book will help you learn everything you need to know about the Ninja Foodi and how it can drastically change your meal times by simply pressing a few buttons.

It provides delicious and healthy recipes that won't take you long time to prepare. Thus, you can feed your family with healthy meals without stressing yourself too much or spending long hours inside the kitchen.

Have fun!

Chapter 1: Why Ninja Foodi?

Ninja Foodi is Your Only Kitchen Gadget

The only kitchen gadget you need, the Ninja Foodi takes the place of several different appliances for a simpler way to prepare meals and a lot less washing to do.

Imagine being able to sauté vegetables, steam rice, and cook the perfect steak in just one pot. That's right. You can prepare a meal that has all your daily nutritional requirements using only one appliance. Even better? You can make desserts like a cobbler and flan in the very same unit.

The Ninja Foodi is not just for cooking food for adults. If you have a little one at home, you can use the Foodi to make healthy and delicious baby food so you know exactly what you're feeding your child.

As you've probably guessed, Ninja Foodi is not your average kitchen appliance because getting one for your home is like getting your own personal chef. Ninja Foodi was developed through the collaboration of the Ninja engineers and a group of chefs who tested the unit at every stage of the product development. The result? Even those who have no prior cooking experience can make flavor-packed meals at home that the whole family will enjoy.

Ninja Foodi Combines Pressure Cooker with Air Fryer

If you look around the market, there is no shortage of kitchen gadgets that combine the slow cooker and pressure cooking functions. That's all well and good, but what if you want something fried and crispy? You'll have to take out either your frying pan or deep fryer to achieve the right crunch and color.

Ninja Foodi is the first to combine a pressure cooker and another very popular kitchen appliance today: the air fryer. This means you can make roast chicken that is juicy and tender within and beautiful bronzed and crisp outside.

How? Ninja Foodi uses super-heated steam to infuse moisture into the food using the pressure cooking function. Then, with the powerful crisping lid, the machine releases rapid-hot air down and all around the food to create the crispy finish characteristic of fried foods without having to use a lot of oil.

Each Ninja Foodi comes with the Cook & Crisp basket, which allows you to cook a 5-pound chicken, 2 pounds if chicken wings, or 3 pounds of French fries.

It Works Automatically

Having a Ninja Foodi is like having a reliable kitchen assistant. For example, you forget that you were cooking something. When the cooking time is over, the Foodi automatically switches to the Keep Warm mode so your food will be the perfect temperature for when you're ready to eat.

The default length of the Keep Warm mode is 12 hours and you'll see the unit counting down. This way, you know how long the Ninja Foodi has been keeping your food warm at a temperature that is safe for consumption.

It Helps Plan Meals Ahead of Time

When you know you only need one kitchen appliance to prepare everything from entree to dessert, meal planning becomes easy.

You can create a weekly schedule of meals that use basically the same ingredients to cut back on your prep time as well as costs.

As an alternative, you can cook big batches of food during the weekend (or whenever you have free time) so you have your meals sorted throughout the week.

Another way to get a head start on your meal prep is to roast a whole chicken or make pulled pork out of boneless pork butt. Set these aside until you are ready to add them to salads, sandwiches, and other dishes like fried rice.

Of course, the pressure cooking function is great to extracting flavor from chicken, pork, or beef bones along with vegetables scraps and make a delicious stock to be used as a soup base for noodles or pasta.

There are so many options. You just need to have a bit of imagination.

365 Meals- All-in-One Pot Meals

If you only have time to cook a complete meal for your family on the weekends, you're not alone. Everyone is so busy these days, there is simply no time to spend even an hour in the kitchen.

With Ninja Foodi, you only need one appliance to create a complete meal so you and your family can enjoy delicious, homecooked food even in the middle of the work week. Do you usually forget to thaw meat before leaving for work in the morning? Not to worry. You can cook food directly from its frozen state. You can also cook grains or beans without having to pre-soak. Talk about convenience!

Some examples of 360 meals you can make with the Ninja Foodi:

>Steak, steamed herbed rice, and sautéed vegetables
>Roast chicken and air-fried potato wedges
>Pot roast and steamed carrots, potatoes, and leeks
>Sausages, puy lentils, and caramelized onions
>Chicken thighs, sweet potato, and red bell pepper with olive oil and Italian herbs

And, remember, you can use Ninja Foodi to make dessert. It can't get any better than that.

It is Healthy for Human Beings

Fried foods are chock-full of calories and fats, which is why most healthy diets recommend that you cut back on your intake of foods cooked in fat if you want to lose weight.

Eating less fried foods is also ideal if you want to have good health in general because frying food can produce compounds like acrylamide, which is classified as a "possible carcinogen," according to the International Agency for Research on Cancer.

One of the reasons air fryers have become so popular is that it is generally regarded as the "healthier" way of frying foods because you use little to no oil to cook food. Consequently, compared to traditional deep-frying air-frying may reduce acrylamide by 90 percent.

While air-frying is better than deep-frying in many ways, it's important to note that air-fried foods are still fried foods. This means they still contain fats and calories that may not be necessarily good for the health, which is why it's not ideal to eat this type of food every day.

It is Quick and Time-Saving

Who wouldn't to eat delicious food every day? But even if you have some free time, you wouldn't want to spend it slaving away in the kitchen.

If you've never had a complete and flavorful meal of juicy chicken thighs, fragrant Basmati rice, and tender-crisp broccoli and carrots, plus a mouthwatering peach cherry crumble in under one hour, the Foodi can make it possible.

You can cook a sumptuous meal while you help your child build a fort or catch up on your reading. The Ninja Foodi takes the guesswork out of the equation to allow you to prepare quick and time-saving meals and still have time to do things that truly matter.

It Uses Less Oil

Ever tried cooking French fries or onion rings the old-fashioned way? Then, you know just how much oil it takes for the food to crisp up perfectly. With the Ninja Foodi, you don't even have to use oil at all. If you want to boost the crunch, a spritz of fat is all you need.

The other benefit of using less oil when cooking is that you don't have to deal with the splatters, which typically happens no matter how much you dry the food prior to cooking.

When you use less oil, you reduce the risk of burning yourself. You also have fewer cleanups to do because there won't be oil stains on your stove, the kitchen counter, or the walls.

In an effort to reduce the use of oil to crisp up foods, many have resorted to using the oven to make vegetable fries or chicken wings. However, foods cooked in the oven tend to dry out. With the Ninja Foodi, the foods are not only crispy they are also moist and tender.

It Saves Energy

If you use your oven in the summer, you know just how hot the kitchen can get. Because it gets very hot, you'll need to up the air-conditioning just so you won't collapse from heat exhaustion.

Cooking with the Ninja Foodi is much more comfortable and energy saving at the same time. The appliance isn't only more efficient than an oven, it won't turn your house into a spa.

It Makes Dishes Tender Inside and Crispy Outside

The Ninja Foodi's pressure cooker and air fryer is a match made in culinary heaven. As a pressure cooker, the Foodi can transform the toughest cuts of meat, frozen vegetables, and even dried grains, beans, and legumes into tender, juicy, and flavorful meals in half the time and with minimal cooking skills.

Say you're cooking a whole roast chicken. The pressure-cooking function ensures that the meat is thoroughly cooked but still moist and full of flavor.

The air frying function, which uses super-heated steam to add another layer of flavor and moisture to the dish, allows you to have chicken with crisp and golden-brown skin without getting anywhere near a deep-fryer.

That's why the Ninja Foodi is one-of-a-kind. You get the benefits of pressure cooking and air frying in one nifty appliance. You'll be looking forward to eating homecooked meals every day and you won't feel the need to eat out ever again!

It can Cook Frozen Ingredients

Having a Ninja Foodi means you won't have to worry about thawing ingredients before cooking them. In 30 minutes, can enjoy perfectly cooked steak or crispy chicken wings.

How? By using the pressure-cooking function to defrost and tenderize the ingredients, then air-frying them afterwards. This means you no longer have to order takeout even if you got home a little late from work.

The Food Will be Nutritional and Delicious

Cooking with the Ninja Foodi lets you create not just delicious and flavorful meals but also nutritional foods as well. This is particularly true with vegetables that are pressure-cooked or steamed.

Compared to traditional stovetop cooking, it takes a short time for this type of food to cook in the Ninja Foodi. Consequently, there is minimal loss of vitamins and nutrients and you get to enjoy vegetables along with all of their goodness.

Other Benefits of Ninja Foodi Cooking

Apart from all the great uses of the Ninja Foodi, the following are some of the other benefits you can enjoy with this gadget:

Produce crunchy topping on food without using an oven - While you can make cakes using pressure cookers on the market, it would be hard to achieve the crispy topping on a cobbler or mac & cheese without the Air Crisp function of the Ninja Foodi.

Create healthy and delicious baby food - Parents who are concerned about the food their babies eat love the Ninja Foodi because it allows them to make baby food from fresh and wholesome ingredients. You can easily tenderize a big batch of fruits, vegetables, and meats so you'll have delicious baby food any day of the week.

Why is it Better Than Instant Pot, Slow Cooker or Air Fryer?

What's better than having a pressure cooker, slow cooker, and air fryer? Having all these functions in one appliance - the Ninja Foodi.

Remember, too, that the Foodi can function as a stovetop because you can use it to sear, sauté, broil, bake, and with some models, dehydrate fruits, vegetables, and meat for healthy and delicious snacks. It will be hard for Instant Pot, Slow Cooker or Air Fryer to top that.

Chapter 2: Ninja Foodi 101

Different Models of Ninja Foodi

Most Ninja Foodi models are 6.5 quarts, which is generally suited to all types of households. However, there is also the 8-quart Ninja Foodi Delux for those who want to be able to cook for a big family or a party.

Inclusions for each model vary, but in general, the Ninja Foodi comes with a ceramic-coated cooking pot, a Cook & Crisp Basket, a stainless steel Reversible Rack, a pressure lid, a crisping lid, and a recipe inspiration guide.

Other models include a Cook & Crisp Layered Insert and a recipe book. You can also purchase the Dehydrating Rack as a separate accessory but check to see if it can work with the Ninja Foodi model you are buying.

Review the Magic of Ninja Foodi One-by-one

Here's a guide to some of the most commonly used functions and buttons of Ninja Foodi:

Function Buttons:

- PRESSURE - The pressure cooker button is used to tenderize food quickly while locking in all the moisture and flavor.
- STEAM - The steam function uses heated water vapor to cook delicate foods gently at a high temperature. This is ideal for perfectly cooking fish and vegetables.
- SLOW COOK - The slow cooker function cooks food at a lower temperature for longer lengths of time. This is great for dishes like pulled pork and fall-off-the-bone pork/beef ribs.
- SEAR/SAUTE - The searing/sautéing function transforms the Ninja Foodi into a stovetop for sautéing vegetables like garlic and onions, simmering sauces, browning meats prior to stewing/braising for more flavor, as well as a host of other uses.
- AIR CRISP - The air-frying function is great for making crisp foods like French fries, zucchini wedges, and onion rings without having to deep-fry them. This function is ideal for making golden-skinned roast chicken or roast pork belly with crackling.

BAKE/ROAST - The baking/roasting function transforms the Ninja Foodi into an oven so you can make baked treats, tender meats, and even pizza with crisp cheesy top.

BROIL - The broiling function allows you to caramelize or brown food. You can do this at the start of the cooking process to caramelize the sugar in meats and vegetables for a more flavorful stew or broth.

DEHYDRATE (Only available in certain models) - The dehydrating function lets you make dehydrated fruits, vegetables, and meats for healthy snacking as well as to increase the shelf life of these food items.

Operating Buttons:

TEMP arrows - The TEMP arrows allow you to adjust the cooking temperature and/or pressure level by pressing the up and down buttons accordingly.

TIME arrows - The TIME arrows allow you to adjust the cooking time using the up and down buttons.

START/STOP - To start cooking, press the START/STOP button after selecting the temperature/pressure and time. To stop the machine's cooking function, press the START/STOP button again.

KEEP WARM - This button automatically switches on after steaming, slow cooking, pressure cooking, or another cooking function is finished. The KEEP WARM mode will stay on for 12 hours. To turn off the mode, just press the KEEP WARM button. The KEEP WARM button keeps food warm at a food safe temperature. In other words, it is not meant to be used to warm food from a cold/frozen state.

POWER - This button shuts off the unit and stops all modes of cooking.

STANDBY MODE: The unit will enter STANDY MODE when there is no interaction with the control panel for 10 minutes.

Steps of Using Ninja Foodi

Before using your Ninja Foodi for the first time, make sure to do the following:

1. Remove all the packaging material, tape, and promotional labels. Discard these using proper segregation protocols.
2. Remove all the accessories from the package.
3. Read the manual, paying special attention to instructions on how to operate the unit, usage warnings, as well as crucial safety tips to prevent damage and injury.
4. Using hot, soapy water, wash the silicone ring, condensation collector, removable cooking pot, Reversible Rack, Cook & Crisp Basket and pressure lid. Rinse and dry these accessories thoroughly. Check the

pressure to make sure no debris is in the valves. IMPORTANT NOTE: Never place the pressure lid or the cooker base in the dishwasher.
5. Place the silicone ring around the outer edge of the silicone ring rack under the lid. Make sure it is completely inserted and that it is lying flat under the silicone ring rack. Before each use, the silicone ring should be well seated in the silicone ring rack and the anti-clog cap must be mounted correctly on the pressure release valve.
6. Install the condensation collector by sliding it into the slot found on the cooker base. To remove, slide it out.

Once you've done all the previous steps, you can begin using your Ninja Foodi. To give you an ideal how easy it is to use the Ninja Foodi, take a look at the following are steps to making ginger rice with marinated chicken:

1. Marinate about 2 lbs. of chicken thighs in soy sauce, lime juice, minced garlic, minced ginger, green onions, and chilies (optional) for at least 30 minutes.
2. Wash a cup of Basmati rice before placing it in the main cooking pot with 1 cup of water, chopped ginger, chopped green onions, a few drops of sesame oil, and some salt.
3. Place the Reversible Rack in the cooking pot on top of the rice. Place the chicken (without the marinade) on the low rack.
4. Place the pressure lid on the Ninja Foodi and turn to lock in place.
5. Press the POWER button, then press PRESSURE. The default temperature is HI.
6. Set the timer to 4 minutes. Then, press the START/STOP button.
7. When the pressure cooking is done, allow the Ninja Foodi to go into KEEP WARM mode for 10 minutes.
8. When the pressure valve is down, remove the pressure lid.
9. Arrange green beans around the chicken and spritz a bit of oil on the surface of the meat and vegetables. Put the air crisping lid down.
10. Press the AIR CRISP button and set the temperature to 400°F for 15 minutes to begin with. Check the doneness of the food mid-way and decide whether to adjust the length of cooking time or not.

Essential Tips and Tricks for Newbies

For most users, the Ninja Foodi will replace the function of many kitchen appliances like the oven or a slow cooker.

To use the Ninja Foodi as an oven:
- Use the BAKE/ROAST function and decrease the cooking temperature by 25°F.
- Make sure to check the food frequently to prevent overcooking.
- It's ideal to use a food thermometer to check the food's internal temperature. This ensures that the food, particularly poultry, is fully cooked before consumption.

To use the Ninja Foodi as a slow cooker:
- Slow cooker recipes are typically cooked for 4 hours on high or 8 hours on low. To use the same recipe with the Foodi, select HI pressure and cook the food for 25-30 minutes with a cup or more of liquid.

To adjust the recipe quantity:
- If cooking more ingredients that a recipe calls for, increase the cooking time. If cooking less, decrease the cooking time.
- Check the ingredients frequently to make sure they don't dry out or overcook.
- Use a food thermometer to check the internal temperature of food prior to consumption.

Additional tips to make the most of the cooking functions:

Pressure cooking - Use hot liquid to build pressure inside the Foodi faster.

Steaming - Give steamed vegetables more texture by using the Cook & Crisp Basket to steam them. Then, spritz the veggies with a little oil and use the air-frying function with the Crisping Lid.

Searing/Sautéing - Before searing meats, leave them out to thaw at room temperature for at least 20-30 minutes. Use a paper towel to pat them dry then set on HI to sear. To simmer sauces, set on LO and for sautéing set on MED.

Air-frying - To ensure consistent browning, arrange ingredients in the Cook & Crisp Basket as evenly as possible.

Cautions You Must Know

The Ninja Foodi is easy and safe to use. However, there are precautions you must take to avoid injury to users or damage to the unit.

1. Before using the unit, check the voltage required and make sure the fittings in your kitchen are compatible.
2. Always keep power cords away from heat sources.
3. Always check the unit before use. Pay particular attention to the silicone ring to make sure it is not broken or deformed and that it is completely fastened. Also, ensure that the unit is free from dried food particles.

4. Place the unit on an even and stable surface to prevent leaks or falls.
5. Keep children and pets away when the Ninja Foodi is in use because some parts of the unit's exterior heats up and may cause burns.
6. When releasing pressure, follow what is recommended by the Ninja Foodi cooking guide.
7. Do not touch or place your hand over the release valve when releasing pressure.
8. Before cleaning the unit and accessories, make sure it has properly cooled down.
9. Perform periodic maintenance to make sure the unit is in top condition.

Ninja Foodi Trouble Shooting

Common issues when using the Ninja Foodi and how to troubleshoot them:

1. The unit is taking a long time to come to pressure.

Cooking time is affected by the temperature or quantity of the ingredients, the current temperature of the cooking pot, and the selected temperature.

If the unit is taking time to build pressure, ensure that the pressure lid is fully locked and that the release valve is in the SEAL position. You should also make sure that the silicone ring is fully seated and that it is flush against the lid.

If you live in a high-altitude area, building pressure may also take longer.

2. I can't take the pressure lid off.

Before the unit is completely depressurized, you will not be able to take the pressure lid off. This is a safety feature to prevent injury. To know that the unit has pressurized, check if the red float valve is up. Depressurize the Foodi by turning the pressure release valve to VENT to quick release the pressurized steam. When the red float valve is down, this means the steam is completely released and that the unit is ready to open. Remember to lift the pressure lid up and away from you.

3. The unit is hissing and not reaching pressure.

Check that the pressure release valve is in the SEAL position. If there are still some hissing sounds, the silicone ring may not be completely in place. To stop the cooking, press the START/STOP button and VENT accordingly. Then, remove the pressure lid and ensure that the silicone ring is inserted fully and that it lies flat under the ring rack.

4. There is a "VENT" error message on the screen.

If you are slow cooking or searing/sautéing, the VENT error message will appear when the pressure release valve is in the SEAL position. To correct this, turn the release valve to VENT and leave it in that position until you're finished cooking.

5. The ingredients were not crispy enough.

The quality of the ingredients as well as the temperature affect the doneness of food. To make sure your food is cooked the way you want, check the food in the middle of cooking. If the food is not crispy enough, cook it longer.

6. How much heat is lost when checking food for doneness?

If you're worried about losing heat when checking the doneness of your food mid-cooking, don't. Ninja Foodi is highly efficient in minimizing heat loss when the unit is opened in the middle of the cooking process. When you close the unit, the cooking pot returns to temperature quicker than a typical oven would.

7. How long does it take for the unit to depressurize?

Depending on how much food or liquid is inside the pot, quick release can take up to 2 minutes while natural release can last up to 20 minutes or longer.

PRESSURE COOKING GUIDE

Ingredient	Weight	Amount of liquid	Accessory	Pressure	Time	Release
Whole chicken	4 - 5 lbs.	1 cup	Cook & Crisp basket	High	25 - 30 mins.	Quick
Ground beef, pork, or turkey	1 - 2 lbs.	1/2 cup	N/A	High	5 mins.	Quick
Pork baby back (cut in thirds)	2-1/2 – 3-1/2 lbs.	1 cup	N/A	High	20 mins.	Quick
Whole beef brisket	3 - 4 lbs.	1 cup	N/A	High	1-1/2 hrs.	Quick
Chuck roast (cut in 1-in. Pieces)	2 lbs.	1 cup	N/A	High	25 mins.	Quick

Hardboiled eggs	1 – 12 pcs.	1/2 cup	N/A	High	4 mins.	Quick
Broccoli (cut in 1/2-in. Florets)	1 head / 4 cups	1/2 cup	Reversible rack in lower position	Low	1 min.	Quick
Butternut squash for soup (peeled, cut in 1-in. Pcs.)	20 oz.	1/2 cup	Reversible rack in lower position	High	5 mins.	Quick
Whole green beans	12 oz.	1/2 cup	Reversible rack in lower position	Low	The time the unit takes to pressurize is long enough to cook this food.	Quick
Sweet potatoes for side dish (peeled and cut in 1-in. cubes)	1 lb.	1/2 cup	N/A	High	1-2 mins.	Quick
Brown rice, short/medium or long grain	1 cup	1-1/4 cups	N/A	High	15 mins.	Natural (10 mins) then Quick
Lentils (green or brown)	1 cup dry	2 cups	N/A	Low	5 mins.	Natural (10 mins) then Quick
Red kidney beans	1 lb., soaked 8–24 hrs.	6 cups	N/A	Low	3 mins.	Natural (10 mins)

| | | | | | | then Quick |

AIR CRISPING COOKING GUIDE (Using the Cook & Crisp Basket)

Ingredient	Amount	Preparation	Oil	Temperature	Cooking Time
Bell peppers for roasting	4 pcs.	Whole	None	400°F	25 – 30 mins.
Carrots	1 lb.	Peeled, cut in 1/2-inch pieces	1 tbsp.	390°F	14 – 16 mins.
Corn on the cob	4 ears, cut in half	Whole ears, husks removed	1 tbsp.	390°F	12 – 15 mins.
Kale (for chips)	6 cups, packed	Torn in pieces, stems removed	None	300°F	9 – 12 mins.
Mushrooms	8 oz.	Rinsed, cut in quarters	1 tbsp.	390°F	7 – 8 mins.
Potatoes, russet	1 lb.	Hand-cut fries, thin	1/2 – 3 tbsp. canola	390°F	20 – 25 mins.
Chicken, whole	1 chicken (3–5 lbs.)	Trussed	Brushed with oil	375°F	55 – 75 mins.
Steaks	2 steaks (8 oz. each)	Whole	None	390°F	10 – 20 mins.
Crab cakes	2 cakes (6–8 oz. each)	None	Brushed with oil	350°F	8 – 12 mins.
Frozen chicken nuggets	1 box (12 oz.)	None	None	390°F	11 – 13 mins.
Frozen mozzarella sticks	1 box (11 oz.)	None	None	375°F	6 – 9 mins.

| Frozen pot stickers | 1 bag (10 count) | None | Toss with 1 tsp. grapeseed oil | 390°F | 11 – 14 mins. |
| Frozen tater tots | 1 lb. | None | None | 360°F | 19 – 21 mins. |

STEAMING GUIDE (Using the Reversible Rack)

Ingredient	Amount	Preparation	Liquid	Cooking Time
Asparagus	1 bunch	Whole	2 cups	7 – 15 mins.
Brussels sprouts	1 lb.	Whole, trimmed	2 cups	8 – 17 mins.
Cabbage	1 head	Cut in half, sliced in 1/2-inch strips, without core	2 cups	6 – 12 mins.
Spinach	1 bag (16 oz.)	Whole leaves	2 cups	3 – 7 mins.
Sugar snap peas	1 lb.	Whole pods, trimmed	2 cups	5 – 8 mins.
Poached eggs	4	In silicone cups or ramekins	1 cup	3 – 6 mins.

FAQs

Answers to some of the frequently asked questions about Ninja Foodi:

1. Is the outside of the Ninja Foodi safe to touch when cooking?

The outside unit of the Ninja Foodi will get hot so be careful when touching anything other than the control panel, the handle on the lid, and the exterior handles.

2. Can I cook pasta in the Ninja Foodi?

Yes, you can cook pasta in the Foodi. Refer to one of the recipes in the Inspiration Guide that comes with the unit.

3. The unit has started pressure cooking. Can I still move it?

No, it is NOT recommended that you move the unit once pressure cooking has started.

4. The display shows "E." What does this mean?

An error message denoted by "E" means the unit is not working properly. If this happens, call Customer Service at 1-877-646-5288.

5. What material is the cooking pot made of?

The cooking pot is made of aluminum with FDA-approved, food-safe, PTFE-free, nonstick ceramic coating.

6. Why the two lids?

The Ninja Foodi has two lids that serve different purposes. The pressure lid allows you to make use of the pressure cooking, steaming, slow cooking, and searing/sautéing functions. The crisping lid, on the other hand, allows you to use the air-frying, baking/roasting, and broiling functions.

7. How do I set the cooking temperature?

To set the cooking temperature, look for the TEMP arrows on the left side of the digital display. Press the up or down buttons until you get the desired temperature. If you want to adjust the temperature during cooking, you can but you won't be able to change the pressure setting when pressure cooking has already started.

8. How do I set the cooking time?

To set the cooking time, look for the TIME arrows on the right side of the digital display. The clock will display HH:MM. You can change the cooking time at any point during cooking.

9. How do I release pressure from the Ninja Foodi?

For quick release, use the tab at the end to slide the pressure release valve to VENT. Remember to turn your face away from the valve to avoid the steam that will escape from it. You will know that all the steam is released when the red float valve drops down. Do not touch or place your hand on top of the valve to keep yourself from getting burned by hot steam.

For natural release, don't do anything when the cooking time is complete. Instead, wait for the unit to naturally release the pressure by itself. The process usually takes up to 20 minutes, but it can be longer depending on how much liquid or food is inside.

10. When using the Air Crisp function, do I need to pre-heat the unit?

Yes, but to pre-heat the unit before air-frying, just add 5 minutes to the total cooking time. Then, allow the unit to come to temperature first before putting in the ingredients.

11. I want to cancel a cooking function. How do I do that?

Pressing either the START/STOP or POWER buttons will cancel the cooking.

12. How do I remove the diffuser from the bottom of the Cook & Crisp Basket?

Grasping the diffuser by the edge and pulling it straight back will allow you to remove it from the Cook & Crisp Basket.

13. How do I clean my Ninja Foodi?

Clean the unit thoroughly after each use. Before cleaning, unplug the unit. Remove all the accessories and the pressure lid.

Use a clean, damp cloth to wipe down the cooker base and control panel. You can clean the crisping lid the same way but make sure you allow the heat shield to cool first.

You should never immerse the cooker base in water or any liquid.

Also, you should never put the cooker base in the dishwasher.

The cooking pot, silicone ring, and steam rack are dishwasher-safe. However, the pressure lid needs to be handwashed in warm, soapy water.

Remember to use a non-abrasive sponge or cloth when cleaning the unit.

14. How often should I clean the silicone ring and how?

It is recommended that you clean the silicone ring after every use. Wash the silicone ring in warm, soapy water. If cleaning the silicone ring in the dishwasher, place it on the top rack.

Chapter 3: Ninja Foodi Shopping and Maintenance

Here are some tips for buying, choosing and taking care of your Ninja Foodi.

Where to Shop for it

People wonder where they can buy the versatile Ninja Foodi.

Ninja Foodi is from the company SharkNinja, an innovation leader in the housewares and kitchenware industry and creator of the familiar household brands like Shark and Ninja.

Since Ninja Foodi is taking the market by storm, it's no wonder many online stores and shops sell this amazing product.

Of course, you can purchase it from the [official website](#) of the company. The company offers at least one year warranty for your multi-cooker.

You have two packages to choose from in buying this product on their websites. These packages differ from the price, warranty and even additional freebies.

Ninja Foodi

- Ninja Foodi 6.5-qt.
- TenderCrisp Cooking Technology
- Pressure & crisping lids
- 4-qt. Cook & Crisp Basket
- Reversible rack
- 45+ recipe book
- 1-year VIP warranty

Ninja Foodi Kitchen Collection

- Ninja Foodi 6.5-qt.
- TenderCrisp Cooking Technology
- Pressure & crisping lids
- 4-qt. Cook & Crisp Basket
- Reversible rack
- 45+ recipe book
- Ninja Express Chop
- Cook & Crisp Layered Insert
- Silicone mitts

- 3-year VIP warranty

There are also other websites where you can buy this product such as:

- [Amazon (http://www.amazon.com)](http://www.amazon.com)
- [KOHL's](http://www.kohl.com) (http://www.kohl.com)
- [Best Buy (http://www.bestbuy.com)](http://www.bestbuy.com)
- [Target](http://www.target.com) (http://www.target.com)

These online retailers also offer their own packages. You can choose to pay monthly or quarterly.

If you would like to shop offline, check out these stores:

- Walmart
- Bed Bath and Beyond
- Westwood

How to Choose Your Suitable Ninja Foodi

There are several factors that you need to consider when buying your Ninja Foodi, and these include:

- Size – The size is your number one concern. See to it that the size of your Ninja Foodi will fit sufficiently the number of people to whom you are cooking for. If you have a large family, you may want to get a bigger cooking device, or buy several Ninja Foodis to save time during meal preparation.
- Package inclusions – Some packages offer additional tools and you would want to check these out before making your final decision.
- Budget – Of course, you need to shop around and compare prices from different stores to get the best value for your money.

How to Maintain it

Here are a couple of maintenance tips that you should keep in mind in order to make your Ninja Foodi last a long time with you:

- The product should be cleaned thoroughly after every use. But make sure that you unplug it before cleaning it.
- The cooker base and the control panel only needed to be wiped by a damped cloth, never immerse it in water or any sort of liquid or put in any dishwasher.
- The cooking pot, steam rack, and removable silicone ring are all dishwasher safe so we don't have to worry we can wash it after we use it.
- To clean the lid (including the pressure release valve and anti-clog cap) hand-wash them in warm, soapy water.

To clean the crisping lid, wipe it down with a wet cloth or paper towel after the heat shield has cooled.

Air-dry all parts after cleaning are complete. If there is food residue stuck on the cooking pot or steam rack, place the pot in the sink, fill it with warm water, and allow it to soak before cleaning it.

Chapter 4: Ninja Foodi Pressure Cooker Recipes

Breakfast Recipes

1. Breakfast Frittata

Serves: 2
Preparation time: 35 minutes

Ingredients:

- 1/4 lb. breakfast sausage, cooked and crumbled
- 4 eggs, beaten
- 1/2 cup cheddar cheese, shredded
- 1 red bell pepper, diced
- 1 green onion, chopped
- Cooking spray

Preparation:

1. Mix the eggs, sausage, cheese, onion and bell pepper.
2. Spray a small baking pan with oil. Pour the egg mixture into the pan.
3. Set the basket inside the Ninja Foodi. Close the crisping lid.
4. Choose air crisp function. Cook at 360 degrees F for 20 minutes.

Serving Suggestion: Sprinkle chopped green onion on top.

Tip: You can also use yellow or green bell pepper to add color to the frittata.

Nutritional Information Per Serving:

Calories 380
Total Fat 27.4g
Saturated Fat 12.0g
Cholesterol 443mg
Sodium 694mg
Total Carbohydrates 2.9g

Dietary Fiber 0.4g
Protein 31.2g
Sugars 1g
Potassium 328mg

2. Egg in Toast

Serves: 1
Preparation time: 15 minutes

Ingredients:

- 1 slice bread
- 1 egg
- Salt and pepper to taste
- Cooking spray

Preparation:

1. Spray a small baking pan with oil. Place the bread inside the pan.
2. Make a hole in the middle of the bread slice.
3. Crack open the egg and put it inside the hole.
4. Cover the Ninja Foodi with the crisping lid. Set it to air crisp.
5. Cook at 330 degrees for 6 minutes. Flip the toast and cook for 3 more minutes.

Serving Suggestion: Sprinkle with dried rosemary on top.

Tip: Aside from the salt and pepper, you can also season the egg with herbs like basil.

Nutritional Information Per Serving:

Calories 92
Total Fat 5.2g
Saturated Fat 1.5g
Cholesterol 164mg
Sodium 123mg
Total Carbohydrate 5g
Dietary Fiber 0.3g
Total Sugars 0.7g
Protein 6.2g
Potassium 69mg

3. Baked Eggs

Serves: 1

Preparation time: 10 minutes

Ingredients:

- Cooking spray
- 1 egg
- 1 tsp. dried rosemary
- Salt and pepper to taste

Preparation:

1. Coat a ramekin with oil. Crack the egg into the ramekin.
2. Season with the rosemary, salt and pepper.
3. Close the crisping lid. Set it to air crisp. Cook at 330 degrees F for 5 minutes.

Serving Suggestion: Serve with toasted bread.

Tip: Try using other herbs to add flavor to the egg.

Nutritional Information Per Serving:

Calories 72
Total Fat 5.1g
Saturated Fat 1.5g
Cholesterol 164mg
Sodium 62mg
Total Carbohydrate 1.2g
Dietary Fiber 0.5g
Total Sugars 0.3g
Protein 5.6g
Potassium 72mg

4. Breakfast Potatoes

Serves: 2
Preparation time: 1 hour and 10 minutes

Ingredients:

- 2 potatoes, scrubbed, rinsed and diced
- 1 tablespoon olive oil
- Salt to taste
- 1/4 teaspoon garlic powder

Preparation:

1. Put the potatoes in a bowl of cold water. Soak for 45 minutes.
2. Pat the potatoes dry with paper towel. Toss in olive oil, salt and garlic powder.

3. Put in the Ninja Foodi basket. Seal the crisping lid. Set it to air crisp.
4. Cook at 400 degrees for 20 minutes. Flip the potatoes halfway through.

Serving Suggestion: Garnish with chopped parsley.

Tip: Cook the potatoes on a single layer. Do not overcrowd.

Nutritional Information Per Serving:

Calories 208
Total Fat 7.2g
Saturated Fat 1.1g
Cholesterol 0mg
Sodium 90mg
Total Carbohydrate 33.7g
Dietary Fiber 5.1g
Total Sugars 2.5g
Protein 3.6g
Potassium 871mg

5. Egg & Turkey Sausage Cups

Serves: 4
Preparation time: 20 minutes

Ingredients:

- 8 tablespoons turkey sausage, cooked and crumbled, divided
- 8 tablespoons frozen spinach, chopped and divided
- 8 teaspoons shredded cheddar cheese, divided
- 4 eggs

Preparation:

1. Add a layer of the sausage, spinach and cheese on each muffin cup.
2. Crack the egg open on top. Seal the crisping lid. Set it to air crisp.
3. Cook at 330 degrees for 10 minutes.

Serving Suggestion: Sprinkle basil and Parmesan on top.

Tip: You can also use Monterey Jack cheese in place of cheddar.

Nutritional Information Per Serving:

Calories 171
Total Fat 13.3g
Saturated Fat 4.7g
Cholesterol 190mg
Sodium 289mg

Total Carbohydrate 0.5g
Dietary Fiber 0.1g
Total Sugars 0.4g
Protein 11.9g
Potassium 161mg

6. Omelette

Serves: 2
Preparation time: 15 minutes

Ingredients:

- 2 eggs
- 1/4 cup milk
- 1 tablespoon red bell pepper, chopped
- 1 slice ham, diced
- 1 tablespoon mushrooms, chopped
- Salt to taste
- 1/4 cup cheese, shredded

Preparation:

1. Whisk the eggs and milk in a bowl. Add the ham and vegetables. Season with the salt.
2. Pour the mixture into a small pan. Place the pan inside the Ninja Foodi basket.
3. Seal the crisping lid. Set it to air crisp. Cook at 350 degrees for 8 minutes.
4. Before it is fully cooked, sprinkle the cheese on top.
5. Coat the beef cubes with the salt and pickling spice.
6. In a skillet over medium heat, pour in the olive oil.

Serving Suggestion: Garnish with chopped green onion.

Tip: Use a combination of cheddar and Mozzarella.

Nutritional Information Per Serving:

Calories 177
Total Fat 11g
Saturated Fat 5.1g
Cholesterol 189mg
Sodium 425mg
Total Carbohydrate 7.1g
Dietary Fiber 1g
Total Sugars 4.8g

Protein 13.1g
Potassium 249mg

7. Cheesy Broccoli Quiche

Serves: 2
Preparation time: 40 minutes

Ingredients:

- 1 cup water
- 2 cups broccoli florets
- 1 carrot, chopped
- 1 cup cheddar cheese, grated
- 1/4 cup Feta cheese, crumbled
- 1/4 cup milk
- 2 eggs
- 1 teaspoon parsley
- 1 teaspoon thyme
- Salt and pepper to taste

Preparation:

1. Pour the water inside the Ninja Foodi. Place the basket inside.
2. Put the carrots and broccoli on the basket. Cover the pot.
3. Set it to pressure. Cook at high pressure for 2 minutes.
4. Release the pressure quickly. Crack the eggs into a bowl and beat.
5. Season with the salt, pepper, parsley and thyme. Put the vegetables on a small baking pan. Layer with the cheese and pour in the beaten eggs Place on the basket.
6. Choose air crisp function. Seal the crisping lid. Cook at 350 degrees for 20 minutes.

Serving Suggestion: Garnish with chopped parsley or chives.

Tip: Try other types of cheese for this recipe.

Nutritional Information Per Serving:

Calories 401
Total Fat 28g
Saturated Fat 16.5g
Cholesterol 242mg
Sodium 688mg
Total Carbohydrate 12.8g
Dietary Fiber 3.3g

Total Sugars 5.8g
Protein 26.2g
Potassium 537mg

8. Bacon & Scrambled Eggs

Serves: 2
Preparation time: 15 minutes

Ingredients:

- 4 strips bacon
- 2 eggs
- 1 tablespoon milk
- Salt and pepper to taste

Preparation:

1. Place the bacon inside the Ninja Foodi. Set it to air crisp.
2. Cover the crisping lid. Cook at 390 degrees for 3 minutes.
3. Flip the bacon and cook for another 2 minutes. Remove the bacon and set aside.
4. Whisk the eggs and milk in a bowl. Season with the salt and pepper.
5. Set the Ninja Foodi to sauté. Add the eggs and cook until firm.

Serving Suggestion: Serve with toasted bread.

Tip: You can add herbs to the egg.

Nutritional Information Per Serving:

Calories 272
Total Fat 20.4g
Saturated Fat 6.7g
Cholesterol 206mg
Sodium 943mg
Total Carbohydrate 1.3g
Dietary Fiber 0g
Total Sugars 0.7g
Protein 19.9g
Potassium 279mg

9. French Toast

Serves: 2
Preparation time: 15 minutes

Ingredients:

- 2 eggs, beaten
- 1/4 cup milk
- 1/4 cup brown sugar
- 1 tablespoon honey
- 1 teaspoon cinnamon
- 1/4 teaspoon nutmeg
- 4 slices wholemeal bread, sliced into strips

Preparation:

1. In a bowl, combine all the ingredients except the bread. Mix well.
2. Dip each strip in the mixture. Place the bread strips on the Ninja Foodi basket.
3. Place basket inside the pot. Cover with the crisping lid. Set it to air crisp.
4. Cook at 320 degrees for 10 minutes.

Serving Suggestion:
Dust with Confectioners' sugar.

Tip:
You can also add berries or serve with oatmeal.

Nutritional Information Per Serving:

Calories 295
Total Fat 6.1g
Saturated Fat 2.1g
Cholesterol 166mg
Sodium 332mg
Total Carbohydrate 49.8g
Dietary Fiber 3.9g
Total Sugars 29.4g
Protein 11.9g
Potassium 112mg

10. Eggs & Veggie Burrito

Serves: 8
Preparation time: 30 minutes

Ingredients:

- 3 eggs, beaten
- Salt and pepper to taste

- Cooking spray
- 8 tortillas
- 2 red bell peppers, sliced into strips
- 1 onion, sliced thinly

Preparation:

1. Beat the eggs in a bowl. Season with the salt and pepper. Set aside.
2. Choose sauté mode in the Ninja Foodi. Spray with the oil. Cook the vegetables until soft. Remove and set aside. Pour in the eggs to the pot. Cook until firm.
3. Wrap the eggs and veggies with tortilla.

Serving Suggestion: Sprinkle top part with cheese.

Tip: You can also add carrot sticks in this recipe.

Nutritional Information Per Serving:

Calories 92
Total Fat 2.5g
Saturated Fat 0.6g
Cholesterol 61mg
Sodium 35mg
Total Carbohydrate 14.4g
Dietary Fiber 2.2g
Total Sugars 2.4g
Protein 3.9g
Potassium 143mg

11. Breakfast Casserole

Serves: 4
Preparation time: 50 minutes

Ingredients:

- Cooking spray
- 1 lb. hash browns
- 1 lb. breakfast sausage, cooked and crumbled
- 1 red bell pepper, diced
- 1 green bell pepper, diced
- 1 onion, diced
- 4 eggs
- Salt and pepper to taste

Preparation:

1. Coat a small baking pan with oil. Place the hash browns on the bottom part.
2. Add the sausage, and then the onion and bell peppers.
3. Place the pan on top of the Ninja Foodi basket. Put the basket inside the pot.
4. Close the crisping lid. Set it to air crisp. Cook at 350 degrees F for 10 minutes.
5. Open the lid. Crack the eggs on top. Cook for another 10 minutes.
6. Season with the salt and pepper.

Serving Suggestion: Garnish with fresh basil leaves.

Tip: Use yellow onion for this recipe.

Nutritional Information Per Serving:

Calories 513
Total Fat 34g
Saturated Fat 9.3g
Cholesterol 173mg
Sodium 867mg
Total Carbohydrate 30g
Dietary Fiber 3.1g
Total Sugars 3.1g
Protein 21.1g
Potassium 761mg

12. Herb & Cheese Frittata

Serves: 4
Preparation time: 25 minutes

Ingredients:

- 4 eggs
- 1/2 cup half and half
- 2 tablespoons parsley, chopped
- 2 tablespoons chives, chopped
- 1/4 cup shredded cheddar cheese
- Salt and pepper to taste

Preparation:

1. Beat the eggs in a bowl. Add the rest of the ingredients and stir well.
2. Pour the mixture into a small baking pan.

3. Place the pan on top of the Ninja Foodi basket.
4. Seal the crisping lid. Set it to air crisp. Cook at 330 degrees F for 15 minutes.

Serving Suggestion: Garnish with fresh cilantro.

Tip: Insert a toothpick into the frittata. If the toothpick comes out clean, it means it is already fully cooked.

Nutritional Information Per Serving:

Calories 132
Total Fat 10.2g
Saturated Fat 5g
Cholesterol 182mg
Sodium 119mg
Total Carbohydrate 1.9g
Dietary Fiber 0.1g
Total Sugars 0.5g
Protein 8.3g
Potassium 121mg

13. Roasted Garlic Potatoes

Serves: 6
Preparation time: 30 minutes

Ingredients:

- 2 lb. baby potatoes, sliced into wedges
- 2 tablespoons olive oil
- 2 teaspoons garlic salt

Preparation:

1. Toss the potatoes in olive oil and garlic salt. Add the potatoes to the Ninja Foodi basket. Seal the crisping lid. Set it to air crisp. Cook at 390 degrees F for 20 minutes.

Serving Suggestion: Sprinkle dried herbs on top.

Tip: You can also use plain salt or garlic powder to season the potatoes.

Nutritional Information Per Serving:

Calories 131
Total Fat 4.8g
Saturated Fat 0.7g
Cholesterol 0mg
Sodium 15mg

Total Carbohydrate 19.5g
Dietary Fiber 3.9g
Total Sugars 0.2g
Protein 4.1g
Potassium 635mg

14. Tofu Scramble

Serves: 4
Preparation time: 30 minutes

Ingredients:

- 2 tablespoons olive oil, divided
- 2 tablespoons soy sauce
- 1/2 cup onion, chopped
- 1 teaspoon turmeric
- 1/2 teaspoon onion powder
- 1/2 teaspoon garlic powder
- 1 block firm tofu, sliced into cubes

Preparation:

2. Mix all the ingredients except the tofu. Soak the tofu in the mixture.
3. Place the tofu in the Ninja Foodi pot. Seal the pot. Cover with the crisping lid.
4. Cook at 370 degrees F for 15 minutes.

Serving Suggestion: Garnish with scallions.

Tip: Press the tofu with paper towel to dry.

Nutritional Information Per Serving:

Calories 90
Total Fat 8g
Saturated Fat 1.2g
Cholesterol 0mg
Sodium 455mg
Total Carbohydrate 3.2g
Dietary Fiber 0.7g
Total Sugars 1.1g
Protein 2.7g
Potassium 93mg

15. Avocado Egg

Serves: 2
Preparation time: 30 minutes

Ingredients:

- 1 avocado, sliced in half and pitted
- 2 eggs
- Salt and pepper to taste
- 1/4 cup cheddar, shredded

Preparation:

1. Crack the egg into the avocado slice. Season with the salt and pepper.
2. Put it on the Ninja Foodi basket. Seal the crisping lid.
3. Set it to air crisp. Cook at 400 degrees F for 15 minutes.
4. Sprinkle with the cheese 3 minutes before it is cooked.

Serving Suggestion: Garnish with fresh parsley.

Tip: You can also use mozzarella cheese for this recipe.

Nutritional Information Per Serving:

Calories 281
Total Fat 23g
Saturated Fat 6g
Cholesterol 178mg
Sodium 158mg
Total Carbohydrates 9g
Dietary Fiber 6g
Protein 11g
Potassium 548mg

16. Butter Melted Broccoli Florets

(Prepping time: 10 minutes\ Cooking time: 8 minutes |For 4 servings)

Ingredients

- 4 tablespoons butter
- Salt and pepper to taste
- 2 pounds broccoli florets
- 1 cup whip cream

Directions

1. Arrange basket in the bottom of your Ninja Foodi and add water

2. Place florets on top of the basket. Lock lid and cook on HIGH pressure for 5 minutes
3. Quick release pressure and transfer florets to the pot itself
4. Season with salt, pepper and add butter
5. Lock crisping lid and Air Crisp on 360 degrees F 3 minutes
6. Transfer to a serving plate. Serve and enjoy!

Nutrition Values (Per Serving)

Calories: 178
Fat: 4g
Carbohydrates: 8g
Protein: 6g

17. The Epic Fried Eggs

(Prepping time: 5 minutes\ Cooking time: 10 minutes |For 2 servings)

Ingredients

- 4 eggs
- 1/4 teaspoon ground black pepper
- 1 teaspoon butter, melted
- 3/4 teaspoon salt

Directions

1. Take a small egg pan and brush it with butter. Beat the eggs in the pan
2. Sprinkle with the ground black pepper and salt. Transfer the egg pan in the pot
3. Lower the air fryer lid. Cook the meat for 10 minutes at 350 F. Serve immediately and enjoy!

Nutrition Values (Per Serving)

Calories: 143
Fat: 10.2g
Carbohydrates: 0.9g
Protein: 11.4g

18. Gentle Keto Butter Fish

(Prepping time: 10 minutes\ Cooking time: 30 minutes |For 6 servings)

Ingredients

- 1 pound salmon fillets

- 2 tablespoons ginger/garlic paste
- 3 green chilies, chopped
- Salt and pepper to taste
- 3/4 cup butter

Directions

1. Season salmon fillets with ginger, garlic paste, salt, pepper
2. Place salmon fillets to Ninja Foodi and top with green chilies and butter
3. Lock lid and BAKE/ROAST for 30 minutes at 360 degrees F
4. Bake for 30 minutes and enjoy!

Nutrition Values (Per Serving)

Calories: 507
Fat: 45g
Carbohydrates: 3g
Protein: 22g

19. Sensational Carrot Puree

(Prepping time: 10 minutes \ Cooking time: 4 minutes |For 4 servings)

Ingredients

- 1 and a 1/2 pound carrots, chopped
- 1 tablespoon of butter at room temperature
- 1 tablespoon of agave nectar
- 1/4 teaspoon of sea salt
- 1 cup of water

Directions

1. Clean and peel your carrots properly. Roughly chop up them into small pieces
2. Add 1 cup of water to your Pot
3. Place the carrots in a steamer basket and place the basket in the Ninja Foodi
4. Lock up the lid and cook on HIGH pressure for 4 minutes. Perform a quick release
5. Transfer the carrots to a deep bowl and use an immersion blender to blend the carrots
6. Add butter, nectar, salt, and puree. Taste the puree and season more if needed. Enjoy!

Nutrition Values (Per Serving)

Calories: 143
Fat: 9g
Carbohydrates: 16g
Protein: 2g

20. Simple Broccoli Florets

(Prepping time: 10 minutes\ Cooking time: 6 minutes |For 4 servings)

Ingredients

- 4 tablespoons butter, melted
- Salt and pepper to taste
- 2 pounds broccoli florets
- 1 cup whipping cream

Directions

1. Place a steamer basket in your Ninja Foodi (bottom part) and add water
2. Place florets on top of the basket and lock lid
3. Cook on HIGH pressure for 5 minutes. Quick release pressure
4. Transfer florets from the steamer basket to the pot. Add salt, pepper, butter, and stir
5. Lock crisping lid and cook on Air Crisp mode for 360 degrees F. Serve and enjoy!

Nutrition Values (Per Serving)

Calories: 178
Fat: 14g
Carbohydrates: 8g
Protein: 5g

21. Awesome Magical 5 Ingredient Shrimp

(Prepping time: 10 minutes\ Cooking time: 15 minutes |For 4 servings)

Ingredients

- 2 tablespoons butter
- 1/2 teaspoon smoked paprika
- 1 pound shrimps, peeled and deveined
- Lemongrass stalks
- 1 red chili pepper, seeded and chopped

Directions

1. Take a bowl and mix all of the ingredients well, except lemongrass and marinate for 1 hour
2. Transfer to Ninja Foodi and lock lid, BAKE/ROAST for 15 minutes at 345 degrees F
3. Once done, serve and enjoy!

Nutrition Values (Per Serving)

Calories: 251
Fat: 10g
Carbohydrates: 3g
Protein: 34g

22. Romantic Mustard Pork

(Prepping time: 10 minutes\ Cooking time: 30 minutes |For 4 servings)

Ingredients

- 2 tablespoons butter
- 2 tablespoons Dijon mustard (Keto-Friendly)
- 4 pork chops
- Salt and pepper to taste
- 1 tablespoon fresh rosemary, coarsely chopped

Directions

1. Take a bowl and add pork chops, cover with Dijon mustard and carefully sprinkle rosemary, salt, and pepper. Let it marinate for 2 hours
2. Add butter and marinated pork chops to your Ninja Foodi pot
3. Lock lid and cook on Low-Medium Pressure for 30 minutes
4. Release pressure naturally over 10 minutes. Take the dish out, serve and enjoy!

Nutrition Values (Per Serving)

Calories: 315
Fat: 26g
Carbohydrates: 1g
Protein: 18g

23. Creative And Easy Lamb Roast

(Prepping time: 10 minutes\ Cooking time: 60 minutes |For 6 servings)

Ingredients

- 2 pounds lamb roast
- 1 cup onion soup
- 1 cup beef broth
- Salt and pepper to taste

Directions

1. Transfer lamb roast to your Ninja Foodi pot. Add onion soup, beef broth, salt, and pepper
2. Lock lid and cook on Medium-HIGH pressure for 55 minutes
3. Release pressure naturally over 10 minutes. Transfer to serving bowl, serve and enjoy!

Nutrition Values (Per Serving)

Calories: 349
Fat: 18g
Carbohydrates: 2.9g
Protein: 39g

24. Crispy Tofu And Mushrooms

(Prepping time: 10 minutes\ Cooking time: 10 minutes |For 2 servings)

Ingredients

- 8 tablespoons parmesan cheese, shredded
- 2 cups fresh mushrooms, chopped
- 2 blocks tofu, pressed and cubed
- Salt and pepper to taste
- 8 tablespoons butter

Directions

1. Take a bowl and mix in tofu, salt, and pepper
2. Set your Ninja Foodi to Saute mode and add seasoned tofu, Saute for 5 minutes
3. Add mushroom, cheese and Saute for 3 minutes. Lock crisping lid and Air Crisp for 3 minutes at 350 degrees F. Transfer to serving plate and enjoy!

Nutrition Values (Per Serving)

Calories: 211
Fat: 18g
Carbohydrates: 2g

Protein: 11g

25. A Hearty Sausage Meal

(Prepping time: 10 minutes\ Cooking time: 20 minutes |For 6 servings)

Ingredients
- 4 whole eggs
- 4 sausages, cooked and sliced
- 2 tablespoons butter
- 1/2 cup mozzarella cheese, grated
- 1/2 cup cream

Directions
1. Take a bowl and mix everything
2. Add egg mix to your Ninja Foodi, top with cheese and sausage slices
3. Lock pressure lid and select "BAKE/ROAST" mode and cook for 20 minutes at 345 degrees F
4. Take it out once done, serve and enjoy!

Nutrition Values (Per Serving)
Calories: 180
Fat: 12g
Carbohydrates: 4g
Protein: 12g

26. Deserving Mushroom Saute

(Prepping time: 10 minutes\ Cooking time: 15 minutes |For 8 servings)

Ingredients
- 1 pound white mushrooms, stems trimmed
- 2 tablespoons unsalted butter
- 1/2 teaspoon salt
- 1/4 cup of water

Directions
1. Quarter medium mushrooms and cut any large mushrooms into eight
2. Put mushrooms, butter, and salt in your Foodi's inner pot
3. Add water and lock pressure lid, making sure to seal the valve
4. Cook on HIGH pressure for 5 minutes, quick release pressure once did

5. Once done, set your pot to Saute mode on HIGH mode and bring the mix to a boil over 5 minutes until all the water evaporates
6. Once the butter/water has evaporated, stir for 1 minute until slightly browned. Enjoy!

Nutrition Values (Per Serving)

Calories: 50
Fat: 4g
Carbohydrates: 2g
Protein: 2g

27. Slightly Zesty Lamb Chops

(Prepping time: 5 minutes \ Cooking time: 40 minutes |For 4 servings)

Ingredients

- 4 tablespoons butter
- 3 tablespoons lemon juice
- 4 lamb chops, with bone
- 2 tablespoons almond flour
- 1 cup picante sauce

Directions

1. Coat chops with almond flour, keep them on the side
2. Set your Ninja Foodi to Saute mode and add butter, chops
3. Saute for 2 minutes, add picante sauce and lemon juice
4. Lock lid and cook on HIGH pressure for 40 minutes. Release naturally and serve, enjoy!

Nutrition Values (Per Serving)

Calories: 284
Fat: 20g
Carbohydrates: 1g
Protein: 24g

28. Bacon And Scrambled Egg

(Prepping time: 10 minutes\ Cooking time: 5-10 minutes |For 2 servings)

Ingredients

- 4 strips bacon
- 2 whole eggs

- 1 tablespoon milk
- Salt and pepper to taste

Directions

1. Add bacon inside your Ninja Foodi. Lock Crisping Lid and set it to Air Crisp mode
2. Cook for 3 minutes at 390 degrees F. Flip and cook for 2 minutes more
3. Remove bacon and keep it on the side. Take a bowl and whisk in eggs and milk
4. Season with salt and pepper. Set your Ninja Foodi to Saute mode
5. Add eggs, cook until firm. Serve and enjoy!

Nutrition Values (Per Serving)

Calories: 272
Fat: 20g
Carbohydrates: 1g
Protein: 19g

29. Delicious Creamy Crepes

(Prepping time: 5 minutes \ Cooking time: 30 minutes |For 4 servings)

Ingredients

- 1 and 1/2 teaspoon Splenda
- 3 organic eggs
- 3 tablespoons coconut flour
- 1/2 cup heavy cream
- 3 tablespoons coconut oil, melted and divided

Directions

1. Take a bowl and mix in 1 and 1/2 tablespoons coconut oil, Splenda, eggs, salt and mix well
2. Beat well until mixed. Add coconut flour and keep beating. Stir in heavy cream, beat well
3. Set your Ninja Foodi to Saute mode and add 1/4 of the mixture
4. Saute for 2 minutes on each side. Repeat until all ingredients are used up. Enjoy!

Nutrition Values (Per Serving)

Calories: 145
Fat: 13g
Carbohydrates: 4g

Protein: 4g

30. Egg Stuffed Avocado Dish

(Prepping time: 10 minutes\ Cooking time: 5 minutes |For 6 servings)

Ingredients

- 1/2 tablespoon fresh lemon juice
- 1 medium ripe avocado, peeled, pitted and chopped
- 6 organic eggs, boiled, peeled and cut in half lengthwise
- Salt to taste
- 1/2 cup fresh watercress, trimmed

Directions

1. Place steamer basket at the bottom of your Ninja Foodie. Add water
2. Add watercress on the basket and lock lid
3. Cook on HIGH pressure for 3 minutes, quick release the pressure and drain the watercress
4. Remove egg yolks and transfer them to a bowl
5. Add watercress, avocado, lemon juice, salt into the bowl and mash with a fork
6. Place egg whites in a serving bowl and fill them with the watercress and avocado dish. Serve!

Nutrition Values (Per Serving)

Calories: 132
Fat: 10g
Carbohydrates: 3g
Protein: 5g

Beef, Pork and Lamb Recipes

1. Beef Stir Fry

Serves: 4
Preparation time: 45 minutes

Ingredients:

- 1 lb. beef sirloin, sliced into strips
- 1 tablespoon vegetable oil
- 1-1/2 lb. broccoli florets
- 1 red bell pepper, sliced into strips
- 1 yellow pepper, sliced into strips
- 1 green bell pepper, sliced into strips
- 1/2 cup onion, sliced into strips

Marinade:

- 1/4 cup of hoisin sauce
- 1 teaspoon sesame oil
- 2 teaspoons garlic, minced
- 1 teaspoon of ground ginger
- 1 tablespoon soy sauce
- 1/4 cup of water

Preparation:

1. Put all the marinade ingredients in a bowl. Divide it in half.
2. Soak the beef in the marinade for 20 minutes. Toss the vegetables in the other half.
3. Place the vegetables in the Ninja Foodi basket. Seal the crisping lid.
4. Select air crisp. Cook at 200 degrees F for 5 minutes.
5. Remove the vegetables and set aside. Put the meat on the basket.
6. Seal and cook at 360 degrees for 6 minutes.

Serving Suggestion: Serve on top of white rice.

Tip: You can marinate the beef longer but put inside the refrigerator.

Nutritional Information Per Serving:

Calories 390
Total Fat 13g
Saturated Fat 3.6g
Cholesterol 102mg
Sodium 618mg
Total Carbohydrate 28.9g
Dietary Fiber 6.8g
Total Sugars 13.1g
Protein 41.3g
Potassium 1244mg

2. Mongolian Beef

Serves: 2
Preparation time: 30 minutes

Ingredients:

1 lb. flank steak, sliced thinly
1/4 cup corn starch

Sauce:

- 2 teaspoon vegetable oil
- 1/2 teaspoon ginger, minced
- 1 tablespoon garlic, minced
- 1/2 cup soy sauce
- 1/2 cup water
- 3/4 cup brown sugar

Preparation:

1. Coat the beef with corn starch. Put in the Ninja Foodi basket.
2. Seal the crisping lid. Set it to air crisp.
3. Cook at 390 degrees F for 10 minutes per side.
4. Remove and set aside. Set the pot to sauté. Add the vegetable oil.
5. Saute the ginger and garlic for 1 minute. Stir in the soy sauce, water and brown sugar.
6. Pour the sauce on top of the beef.

Serving Suggestion: Serve with steamed green beans.
Tip: Check the steak every 5 minutes for doneness.

Nutritional Information Per Serving:

Calories 399
Total Fat 11.7g
Saturated Fat 4.4g
Cholesterol 62mg
Sodium 1870mg
Total Carbohydrate 39g
Dietary Fiber 0.3g
Total Sugars 27g
Protein 33.7g
Potassium 500mg

3. Beef & Broccoli

Serves: 6
Preparation time: 40 minutes

Ingredients:

- 1-1/2 lb. beef chuck roast (boneless), trimmed and sliced thinly
- Salt and pepper to taste
- 2 teaspoons olive oil
- 1 onion, chopped
- 4 cloves garlic, minced
- 3/4 cup beef broth
- 1/2 cup soy sauce
- 1/3 cup brown sugar
- 2 tablespoons sesame oil
- 1 lb. broccoli florets
- 3 tablespoons water
- 3 tablespoons corn starch

Preparation:

1. Season the beef strips with salt and pepper.
2. Add the olive oil to the Ninja Foodi. Switch it to sauté.
3. Add the onion and cook for 1 minute. Add the garlic and cook for 30 seconds.
4. Add the beef and cook in batches until brown on both sides.
5. Deglaze the pot with the broth and soy sauce.
6. Stir in the sugar and sesame oil. Cover the pot.
7. Set it to pressure. Cook at high pressure for 12 minutes.

8. Release the pressure naturally. Stir in the broccoli. Seal the pot.
9. Cook at high pressure for 3 minutes. Release the pressure quickly.
10. Stir in the corn starch dissolved in water. Simmer until the sauce has thickened.

Serving Suggestion: Garnish with toasted sesame seeds.

Tip: Use low sodium soy sauce.

Nutritional Information Per Serving:

Calories 563
Total Fat 38.1g
Saturated Fat 13.5g
Cholesterol 117mg
Sodium 1395mg
Total Carbohydrate 20.7g
Dietary Fiber 2.6g
Total Sugars 10.4g
Protein 34.1g
Potassium 616mg

4. Beef Stew

Serves: 4
Preparation time: 50 minutes

Ingredients:

- 1 tablespoon olive oil
- 1-1/2 lb. beef stew meat, sliced into cubes
- 1 teaspoon Italian seasoning
- Salt and pepper to taste
- 2 tablespoons Worcestershire sauce
- 1 onion, chopped
- 3 cloves garlic, minced
- 1 lb. potatoes, cubed
- 16 oz. baby carrots, sliced into cubes
- 10 oz. tomato sauce
- 2-1/2 cups beef broth
- 2 tablespoons corn starch
- 2 tablespoons water

Preparation:

1. Set the Ninja Foodi to sauté. Pour in the oil. Add the beef.

2. Season with the Italian seasoning, salt and pepper. Cook until brown.
3. Add the rest of the ingredients. Cover the pot.
4. Set it to pressure. Cook at high pressure for 35 minutes.
5. Release the pressure naturally. Stir in the corn starch dissolved in water.
6. Switch to sauté and simmer for 3 minutes or until the sauce has thickened.

Serving Suggestion: Serve with crusty bread.

Tip: Skip the potatoes and carrots for a low carb dish.

Nutritional Information Per Serving:

Calories 508
Total Fat 15.6g
Saturated Fat 4.9g
Cholesterol 153mg
Sodium 1052mg
Total Carbohydrate 31.7g
Dietary Fiber 4.4g
Total Sugars 7.5g
Protein 57.9g
Potassium 1560mg

5. Asian Beef

Serves: 6
Preparation time: 30 minutes

Ingredients:

- 1/4 cup soy sauce
- 1/2 cup beef broth
- 1 tablespoon sesame oil
- 1/4 cup brown sugar, packed
- 4 cloves garlic, minced
- 1 teaspoon hot sauce
- 1 tablespoon rice wine vinegar
- 1 tablespoon ginger, grated
- 1/2 teaspoon onion powder
- 1/2 teaspoon pepper
- 3 lb. boneless beef chuck roast, sliced into cubes
- 3 tablespoons corn starch dissolved in 1 teaspoon water

Preparation:
1. Mix all the ingredients in a large bowl except the chuck roast and corn starch.
2. Pour the mixture into the Ninja Foodi. Add the beef. Seal the pot.
3. Select pressure. Cook at high pressure for 15 minutes.
4. Do a quick pressure release. Stir in the corn starch.
5. Select sauté setting to thicken the sauce.

Serving Suggestion: Sprinkle sesame seeds on top.

Tip: You can also use flank steak for this recipe.

Nutritional Information Per Serving:
Calories 482
Total Fat 16.6g
Saturated Fat 5.7g
Cholesterol 203mg
Sodium 836mg
Total Carbohydrate 8.4g
Dietary Fiber 0.3g
Total Sugars 6.2g
Protein 70.1g
Potassium 987mg

6. Pork Chops in Honey Mustard Sauce

Serves: 4
Preparation time: 45 minutes

Ingredients:
- 2 tablespoons honey
- 4 tablespoons mustard
- 2 tablespoons garlic, minced
- Salt and pepper to taste
- 4 pork chops
- Cooking spray

Preparation:
1. Mix the honey, mustard, garlic, salt and pepper in a bowl.
2. Marinate the pork chops in the mixture for 20 minutes.
3. Place the pork chops on the Ninja Foodi basket.
4. Put the basket inside the pot. Seal with the crisping lid.

5. Set it to air crisp. Cook at 350 degrees F for 12 minutes, flipping halfway through.

Serving Suggestion: Serve with rice or noodles.

Tip: You can also use olive oil instead of cooking spray.

Nutritional Information Per Serving:

Calories 348
Total Fat 23.3g
Saturated Fat 7.6g
Cholesterol 69mg
Sodium 58mg
Total Carbohydrate 14g
Dietary Fiber 1.8g
Total Sugars 9.4g
Protein 21.1g
Potassium 374mg

7. Crispy Pork Chops

Serves: 6
Preparation time: 30 minutes

Ingredients:

- Cooking spray
- 6 pork chops
- Salt and pepper to taste
- 1/2 cup bread crumbs
- 2 tablespoons Parmesan cheese, grated
- 1/4 cup cornflakes, crushed
- 1-1/4 teaspoon sweet paprika
- 1/2 teaspoon onion powder
- 1/2 teaspoon garlic powder
- 1/4 teaspoon chili powder
- 1 egg, beaten

Preparation:

1. Season the pork chops with salt and pepper.
2. In a bowl, mix the rest of the ingredients except the egg.
3. Beat the egg in a bowl. Dip the pork chops in the egg.
4. Coat the pork with the breading. Place the pork on the Ninja Foodi basket.
5. Set it to air crisp and close the crisping lid.

6. Cook at 400 degrees F for 12 minutes, flipping halfway through.

Serving Suggestion: Serve with mashed potatoes and gravy.

Tip: You can also use pork cutlets for this recipe.

Nutritional Information Per Serving:

Calories 310
Total Fat 21.3g
Saturated Fat 7.8g
Cholesterol 96mg
Sodium 142mg
Total Carbohydrate 8.2g
Dietary Fiber 0.7g
Total Sugars 0.9g
Protein 20.3g
Potassium 322mg

8. Garlic Butter Pork

Serves: 2
Preparation time: 1 hour and 30 minutes

Ingredients:

- 1 tablespoon coconut butter
- 1 tablespoon coconut oil
- 2 teaspoons cloves garlic, grated
- 2 teaspoons parsley
- Salt and pepper to taste
- 4 pork chops, sliced into strips

Preparation:

1. Combine all the ingredients except the pork strips. Mix well.
2. Marinate the pork in the mixture for 1 hour. Put the pork on the Ninja Foodi basket.
3. Set it inside the pot. Seal with the crisping lid. Choose air crisp function.
4. Cook at 400 degrees for 10 minutes.

Serving Suggestion: Serve with fresh garden salad.

Tip: You can also use pork loin for this recipe.

Nutritional Information Per Serving:

Calories 388
Total Fat 23.3g

Saturated Fat 10.4g
Cholesterol 69mg
Sodium 57mg
Total Carbohydrate 0.5g
Dietary Fiber 0.1g
Total Sugars 0g
Protein 18.1g
Potassium 285mg

9. Pork with Gravy

Serves: 5
Preparation time: 40 minutes

Ingredients:

- 5 pork chops
- 1 tablespoon olive oil
- 1 teaspoon salt
- 1/2 teaspoon pepper
- 1/2 teaspoon garlic powder
- 2 cups beef broth
- 1 packet ranch dressing mix
- 10-1/2 oz. cream of chicken soup
- 1 packet brown gravy mix
- 2 tablespoons corn starch dissolved in 2 tablespoons water

Preparation:

1. Season both sides of the pork chops with salt, pepper and garlic powder.
2. Pour the olive oil into the Ninja Foodi. Set it to sauté.
3. Brown the pork chops on both sides. Remove and set aside.
4. Pour the beef broth to deglaze the pot.
5. Add the rest of the ingredients except the corn starch. Seal the pot.
6. Set it to pressure. Cook at high pressure for 8 minutes. Release the pressure naturally.
7. Remove the pork chops. Turn the pot to sauté. Stir in the corn starch.
8. Simmer to thicken. Pour the gravy over the pork chops.

Serving Suggestion: Serve with mashed potatoes.

Tip: If cream of chicken is not available, you can also use cream of mushroom soup.

Nutritional Information Per Serving:

Calories 357

Total Fat 26.8g
Saturated Fat 9g
Cholesterol 74mg
Sodium 1308mg
Total Carbohydrate 6g
Dietary Fiber 0.1g
Total Sugars 0.8g
Protein 21.6g
Potassium 396mg

10. Hawaiian Pork

Serves: 8
Preparation time: 45 minutes

Ingredients:

- 20 oz. pineapple chunks, undrained
- 2 tablespoons water
- 1 tablespoon corn starch
- 2 tablespoons soy sauce
- 3 tablespoons honey
- 1 tablespoon ginger, grated
- 2 tablespoons brown sugar
- 3 cloves garlic, minced
- 2 tablespoons olive oil, divided
- 1 onion, chopped
- 2 lb. pork stew meat
- Salt and pepper to taste
- 1 teaspoon oregano

Preparation:

1. Mix the pineapple juice, soy sauce, honey, ginger, sugar and garlic in a bowl. Set aside. Set the Ninja Foodi to sauté. Add half of the oil. Cook the onion for 1 minute.
2. Add the remaining oil. Brown the pork on both sides.
3. Add the pineapple chunks, oregano and pineapple juice mixture.
4. Cover the pot. Set it to pressure. Cook at high pressure for 10 minutes.
5. Release the pressure naturally.

Serving Suggestion: Garnish with chopped parsley.
Tip: You can also add red pepper to this recipe.

Nutritional Information Per Serving:

Calories 384
Total Fat 27g
Saturated Fat 9g
Cholesterol 81mg
Sodium 317mg
Total Carbohydrates 13g
Sugars 10g
Protein 20g
Potassium 390mg

11. Middle Eastern Lamb Stew

Serves: 4
Preparation time: 1 hour and 30 minutes

Ingredients:

- 2 tablespoons olive oil
- 1-1/2 lb. lamb stew meat, sliced into cubes
- 1 onion, diced
- 6 garlic cloves, chopped
- 1 teaspoon cumin
- 1 teaspoon coriander
- 1 teaspoon turmeric
- 1 teaspoon cinnamon
- Salt and pepper to taste
- 2 tablespoons tomato paste
- 1/4 cup red wine vinegar
- 2 tablespoons honey
- 1-1/4 cups chicken broth
- 15 oz. chickpeas, rinsed and drained
- 1/4 cup raisins

Preparation:

1. Choose sauté function in the Ninja Foodi. Add the oil. Cook the onion for 3 minutes.
2. Add the lamb and seasonings. Cook for 5 minutes, stirring frequently.
3. Stir in the rest of the ingredients. Cover the pot. Set it to pressure.
4. Cook at high pressure for 50 minutes. Release the pressure naturally.

Serving Suggestion: Serve with quinoa.

Tip: Freeze and serve the next day for a more intense flavor.

Nutritional Information Per Serving:

Calories 867
Total Fat 26.6g
Saturated Fat 6.3g
Cholesterol 153mg
Sodium 406mg
Total Carbohydrate 87.4g
Dietary Fiber 20.4g
Total Sugars 27.9g
Protein 71.2g
Potassium 1815mg

12. Lamb Curry

Serves: 6
Preparation time: 1 hour and 30 minutes

Ingredients:

- 1-1/2 lb. lamb stew meat, cubed
- 1 tablespoon lime juice
- 4 cloves garlic, minced
- 1/2 cup coconut milk
- 1-inch piece fresh ginger, grated
- Salt and pepper to taste
- 1 tablespoon coconut oil
- 14 oz. diced tomatoes
- 3/4 teaspoon turmeric
- 1 tablespoon curry powder
- 1 onion, diced
- 3 carrots, sliced

Preparation:

1. In a bowl, toss the lamb meat in lime juice, garlic, coconut milk, ginger, salt and pepper. Marinate for 30 minutes.
2. Put the meat with its marinade and the rest of the ingredients in the Ninja Foodi.
3. Mix well. Seal the pot. Set it to pressure. Cook at high pressure for 20 minutes.
4. Release the pressure naturally.

Serving Suggestion: Garnish with chopped cilantro.
Tip: Use freshly squeezed lime juice.

Nutritional Information Per Serving:

Calories 631
Total Fat 31.4g
Saturated Fat 18.4g
Cholesterol 204mg
Sodium 230mg
Total Carbohydrate 19.7g
Dietary Fiber 5.7g
Total Sugars 9.5g
Protein 67.2g
Potassium 1490mg

13. Mediterranean Lamb Roast

Serves: 4
Preparation time: 1 hour and 40 minutes

Ingredients:

- 2 tablespoons olive oil
- 5 lb. leg of lamb
- Salt and pepper to taste
- 1 teaspoon dried marjoram
- 3 cloves garlic, minced
- 1 teaspoon dried sage
- 1 teaspoon dried thyme
- 1 teaspoon ground ginger
- 1 bay leaf, crushed
- 2 cups broth
- 3 lb. potatoes, sliced into cubes
- 2 tablespoons arrowroot powder
- 1/3 cup water

Preparation:

1. Set the Ninja Foodi to sauté. Pour in the olive oil. Add the lamb.
2. Coat with the oil. Season with the herbs and spices. Sear on both sides.
3. Pour in the broth. Add the potatoes. Close the pot. Set it to pressure.
4. Cook at high pressure for 50 minutes. Release the pressure naturally.
5. Dissolve the arrowroot powder in water.

6. Stir in the diluted arrowroot powder into the cooking liquid.
7. Let sit for a few minutes before serving.

Serving Suggestion: Serve with cauliflower rice.

Tip: You can use flour or other thickener in place of the arrowroot powder.

Nutritional Information Per Serving:

Calories 688
Total Fat 24.8g
Saturated Fat 8.1g
Cholesterol 255mg
Sodium 417mg
Total Carbohydrate 27.7g
Dietary Fiber 4.2g
Total Sugars 2.2g
Protein 83.8g
Potassium 1705mg

14. Braised Lamb Shanks

Serves: 4
Preparation time: 1 hour and 40 minutes

Ingredients:

- 2 tablespoons olive oil
- 4 lamb shanks
- Salt and pepper to taste
- 4 cloves garlic, minced
- 3/4 cup dry red wine
- 1 teaspoon dried basil
- 3/4 teaspoons dried oregano
- 28 oz. crushed tomatoes

Preparation:

1. Turn the Ninja Foodi to sauté. Add the oil. Season the lamb with salt and pepper.
2. Cook until brown. Remove and set aside. Add the garlic and cook for 15 seconds.
3. Pour in the wine. Simmer for 2 minutes. Stir in the basil, oregano and tomatoes.
4. Put the lamb back to the pot. Seal the pot. Set it to pressure.
5. Cook at high pressure for 45 minutes. Release the pressure naturally.

Serving Suggestion: Serve over polenta.

Nutritional Information Per Serving:

Calories 790
Total Fat 31g
Saturated Fat 9.6g
Cholesterol 294mg
Sodium 632mg
Total Carbohydrate 18.3g
Dietary Fiber 6.5g
Total Sugars 11.5g
Protein 96.8g
Potassium 1157mg

15. Rosemary Lamb Chops

Serves: 6
Preparation time: 20 minutes

Ingredients:

- 3 lb. lamb chops
- 4 rosemary sprigs
- Salt to taste
- 1 tablespoon olive oil
- 2 tablespoons butter
- 1 tablespoon tomato paste
- 1 cup beef stock
- 1 green onion, sliced

Preparation:

1. Season the lamb chops with rosemary, salt and pepper.
2. Pour in the olive oil and add the butter to the Ninja Foodi. Set it to sauté.
3. Add the lamb chops and cook for one minute per side. Add the rest of the ingredients.
4. Stir well. Cover the pot. Set it to pressure. Cook at high pressure for 5 minutes.
5. Release the pressure naturally.

Serving Suggestion: Serve with pickled onions.

Tip: You can also use tomato sauce in place of tomato paste.

Nutritional Information Per Serving:

Calories 484
Total Fat 23g
Saturated Fat 8.8g
Cholesterol 214mg
Sodium 361mg
Total Carbohydrate 1.2g
Dietary Fiber 0.5g
Total Sugars 0.4g
Protein 64.4g
Potassium 824mg

16. Tantalizing Beef Jerky

(Prepping time: 10 minutes\ Cooking time: 20 minutes |For 4 servings)

Ingredients

- 1/2 pound beef, sliced into 1/8 inch thick strips
- 1/2 cup of soy sauce
- 2 tablespoons Worcestershire sauce
- 2 teaspoons ground black pepper
- 1 teaspoon onion powder
- 1/2 teaspoon garlic powder
- 1 teaspoon salt

Directions

1. Add listed ingredient to a large-sized Ziploc bag, seal it shut
2. Shake well, leave it in the fridge overnight
3. Lay strips on dehydrator trays, making sure not to overlap them
4. Lock Air Crisping Lid and set the temperature to 135 degrees F, cook for 7 hours
5. Store in airtight container, enjoy!

Nutrition Values (Per Serving)

Calories: 62
Fat: 7g
Carbohydrates: 2g
Protein: 9g

17. Beefed Up Spaghetti Squash

(Prepping time: 5 minutes\ Cooking time: 10-15 minutes |For 4 servings)

Ingredients

- 2 pounds ground beef
- 1 medium spaghetti squash
- 32 ounces marinara sauce
- 3 tablespoons olive oil

Directions

1. Slice squash in half lengthwise and dispose of seeds
2. Add trivet to your Ninja Foodi
3. Add 1 cup water
4. Arrange squash on the rack and lock lid, cook on HIGH pressure for 8 minutes
5. Quick release pressure
6. Remove from pot
7. Clean pot and set your Ninja Foodi to Saute mode
8. Add ground beef and add olive oil, let it heat up
9. Add ground beef and cook until slightly browned and cooked
10. Separate strands from cooked squash and transfer to a bowl
11. Add cooked beef, and mix with marinara sauce. Serve and enjoy!

Nutrition Values (Per Serving)

Calories: 174
Fat: 6g
Carbohydrates: 5g
Protein: 19g

18. Adobo Cubed Steak

(Prepping time: 5 minutes\ Cooking time: 25 minutes |For 4 servings)

Ingredients

- 2 cups of water
- 8 steaks, cubed, 28 ounces pack
- Pepper to taste
- 1 and 3/4 teaspoons adobo seasoning
- 1 can (8 ounces) tomato sauce
- 1/3 cup green pitted olives

- 2 tablespoons brine
- 1 small red pepper
- 1/2 a medium onion, sliced

Directions

1. Chop peppers, onions into ¼ inch strips
2. Prepare beef by seasoning with adobo and pepper
3. Add into Ninja Foodi
4. Add remaining ingredients and Lock lid, cook on HIGH pressure for 25 minutes
5. Release pressure naturally
6. Serve and enjoy!

Nutrition Values (Per Serving)

Calories: 154
Fat: 5g
Carbohydrates: 3g
Protein: 23g

19. Cool Beef Bourguignon

(Prepping time: 10 minutes\ Cooking time: 30 minutes |For 4 servings)

Ingredients

- 1 pound stewing steak
- 1/2 pound bacon
- 5 medium carrots, diced
- 1 large red onion, peeled and sliced
- 2 garlic cloves, minced
- 2 teaspoons salt
- 2 tablespoons fresh thyme
- 2 tablespoons fresh parsley
- 2 teaspoons ground pepper
- 1/2 cup beef broth
- 1 tablespoon olive oil
- 1 tablespoon sugar-free maple syrup (Keto friendly)

Directions

1. Set your Ninja Foodi to Saute mode and add 1 tablespoon of oil, allow the oil to heat up
2. Pat your beef dry and season it well

3. Add beef into the Ninja Foodi (in batches) and Saute them until nicely browned up
4. Slice up the cooked bacon into strips and add the strips to the pot
5. Add onions as well and brown them
6. Add the rest of the listed ingredients and lock up the lid
7. Cook for 30 minutes on HIGH pressure
8. Allow the pressure to release naturally over 10 minutes. Enjoy!

Nutrition Values (Per Serving)

Calories: 416
Fats: 18g
Carbs: 12g
Protein:27g

20. A Keto-Friendly Philly Willy Steak And Cheese

(Prepping time: 10 minutes\ Cooking time: 40 minutes |For 4 servings)

Ingredients

- 2 tablespoons olive oil
- 2 large onion, sliced
- 8 ounces mushrooms, sliced
- 1-2 teaspoons Keto friendly steak seasoning
- 1 tablespoon butter
- 2 pounds beef chuck roast
- 12 cup beef stock

Directions

1. Set your Ninja Foodi to Saute mode and add oil, let it heat up
2. Rub seasoning over roast and Saute for 1-2 minutes per side
3. Remove and add butter, onion
4. Add mushrooms, pepper, stock, and roast
5. Lock lid and cook on HIGH pressure for 35 minutes
6. Naturally, release pressure over 10 minutes
7. Shred meat and sprinkle cheese if using, enjoy!

Nutrition Values (Per Serving)

Calories: 425
Fats: 25g
Carbs: 3g
Protein: 46g

21. Beef Stew

(Prepping time: 10 minutes\ Cooking time: 10 minutes |For 4 servings)

Ingredients

- 1 pound beef roast
- 4 cups beef broth
- 3 garlic cloves, chopped
- 1 carrot, chopped
- 2 celery stalks, chopped
- 2 tomatoes, chopped
- 1/2 white onion, chopped
- 1/4 teaspoon salt
- 1/8 teaspoon ground black pepper

Directions

1. Add listed ingredients to your Ninja Foodi and lock lid, cook on HIGH pressure for 10 minutes
2. Quick release pressure. Open the lid and shred the bee using forks, serve and enjoy!

Nutrition Values (Per Serving)

Calories: 211
Fat: 7g
Carbohydrates: 2g
Protein: 10g

22. Juiciest Keto Bacon Strips

(Prepping time: 5 minutes\ Cooking time: 7 minutes |For 2 servings)

Ingredients

- 10 bacon strips
- 1/4 teaspoon chili flakes
- 1/3 teaspoon salt
- 1/4 teaspoon basil, dried

Directions

1. Rub the bacon strips with chili flakes, dried basil, and salt
2. Turn on your air fryer and place the bacon on the rack
3. Lower the air fryer lid. Cook the bacon at 400F for 5 minutes
4. Cook for 3 minutes more if the bacon is not fully cooked. Serve and enjoy!

Nutrition Values (Per Serving)

Calories: 500
Fat: 46g
Carbohydrates: 0g
Protein: 21g

23. Quick Picadillo Dish

(Prepping time: 10 minutes\ Cooking time: 15-20 minutes |For 4 servings)

Ingredients

- 1/2 pound lean ground beef
- 2 garlic cloves, minced
- 1/2 large onion, chopped
- 1 teaspoon salt
- 1 tomato, chopped
- 1/2 red bell pepper, chopped
- 1 tablespoon cilantro
- 1/2 can (4 ounces) tomato sauce
- 1 teaspoon ground cumin
- 1-2 bay leaves
- 2 tablespoons green olives, capers
- 2 tablespoons brine
- 3 tablespoons water

Directions

1. Set your Ninja Foodi to Saute mode and add meat, salt, and pepper, slightly brown
2. Add garlic, tomato, onion, cilantro and Saute for 1 minute. Add olives, brine, leaf, cumin, and mix
3. Pour in sauce, water, and stir. Lock lid and cook on HIGH pressure for 15 minutes
4. Quick release pressure

Nutrition Values (Per Serving)

Calories: 207
Fats: 8g
Carbs: 4g
Protein: 25g

24. Simple/Aromatic Meatballs

(Prepping time: 8 minutes\ Cooking time: 11 minutes |For 4 servings)

Ingredients

- 2 cups ground beef
- 1 egg, beaten
- 1 teaspoon Taco seasoning
- 1 tablespoon sugar-free marinara sauce
- 1 teaspoon garlic, minced
- 1/2 teaspoon salt

Directions

1. Take a big mixing bowl and place all the ingredients into the bowl
2. Add all the ingredients into the bowl. Mix together all the ingredients by using a spoon or fingertips. Then make the small size meatballs and put them in a layer in the air fryer rack
3. Lower the air fryer lid. Cook the meatballs for 11 minutes at 350 F. Serve immediately and enjoy!

Nutrition Values (Per Serving)

Calories: 205
Fat: 12.2g
Carbohydrates: 2.2g
Protein: 19.4g

25. Generous Shepherd's Pie

(Prepping time: 10 minutes\ Cooking time: 10-15 minutes |For 4 servings)

Ingredients

- 2 cups of water
- 4 tablespoons butter
- 4 ounces cream cheese
- 1 cup mozzarella
- 1 whole egg
- Salt and pepper to taste
- 1 tablespoon garlic powder
- 2-3 pounds ground beef
- 1 cup frozen carrots
- 8 ounces mushrooms, sliced

- 1 cup beef broth

Directions

1. Add water to Ninja Foodi, arrange cauliflower on top, lock lid and cook for 5 minutes on HIGH pressure. Quick release and transfer to a blender, add cream cheese, butter, mozzarella cheese, egg, pepper, and salt. Blend well. Drain water from Ninja Foodi and add beef
2. Add carrots, garlic powder, broth and pepper, and salt
3. Add in cauliflower mix and lock lid, cook for 10 minutes on HIGH pressure
4. Release pressure naturally over 10 minutes. Serve and enjoy!

Nutrition Values (Per Serving)

Calories: 303
Fats: 21g
Carbs: 4g
Protein: 21g

26. Hybrid Beef Prime Roast

(Prepping time: 10 minutes\ Cooking time: 45 minutes |For 4 servings)

Ingredients

- 2 pounds chuck roast
- 1 tablespoon olive oil
- 1 teaspoon salt
- 1 teaspoon ground black pepper
- 1 teaspoon onion powder
- 1 teaspoon garlic powder
- 4 cups beef stock

Directions

1. Place roast in Ninja Food pot and season it well with salt and pepper
2. Add oil and set the pot to Saute mode, sear each side of roast for 3 minutes until slightly browned
3. Add beef broth, onion powder, garlic powder, and stir
4. Lock lid and cook on HIGH pressure for 40 minutes
5. Once the timer goes off, naturally release pressure over 10 minutes
6. Open the lid and serve hot. Enjoy!

Nutrition Values (Per Serving)

Calories: 308
Fat: 22g

Carbohydrates: 2g
Protein: 24g

27. The Epic Carne Guisada

(Prepping time: 10 minutes\ Cooking time: 45 minutes |For 4 servings)

Ingredients

- 3 pounds beef stew
- 3 tablespoon seasoned salt
- 1 tablespoon oregano chili powder
- 1 tablespoon organic cumin
- 1 pinch crushed red pepper
- 2 tablespoons olive oil
- 1/2 medium lime, juiced
- 1 cup beef bone broth
- 3 ounces tomato paste
- 1 large onion, sliced

Directions

1. Trim the beef stew as needed into small bite-sized portions
2. Toss the beef stew pieces with dry seasoning
3. Set your Ninja Foodi to Saute mode and add oil, allow the oil to heat up
4. Add seasoned beef pieces and brown them
5. Combine the browned beef pieces with rest of the ingredients
6. Lock up the lid and cook on HIGH pressure for 3 minutes
7. Release the pressure naturally
8. Enjoy!

Nutrition Values (Per Serving)

Protein: 33g
Carbs: 11g
Fats: 12g
Calories: 274

28. No-Noodle Pure Lasagna

(Prepping time: 10 minutes\ Cooking time: 10-15 minutes |For 4 servings)

Ingredients

- 2 small onions
- 2 garlic cloves, minced

- 1 pound ground beef
- 1 large egg
- 1 and 1/2 cups ricotta cheese
- 1/2 cup parmesan cheese
- 1 jar (25 ounces0 marinara sauce
- 8 ounces mozzarella cheese, sliced

Directions

1. Set your Ninja Foodi to Saute mode add beef, brown the beef
2. Add onion and garlic
3. Add parmesan, ricotta, egg in a small dish and keep it on the side
4. Add sauce to browned meat, reserve half for later
5. Sprinkle mozzarella and half of ricotta cheese to the browned meat
6. Top with remaining meat sauce
7. For the final layer, add more mozzarella cheese and remaining ricotta
8. Stir well
9. Cover with foil transfer to Ninja Foodi
10. Lock lid and cook on HIGH pressure for 8-10 minutes
11. Quick release pressure
12. Drizzle parmesan cheese on top
13. Enjoy!

Nutrition Values (Per Serving)

Calories: 365
Fats: 25g
Carbs: 6g
Protein: 25g

29. The Wisdom Worthy Corned Beef

(Prepping time: 10 minutes\ Cooking time: 60 minutes |For 4 servings)

Ingredients

- 4 pounds beef brisket
- 2 garlic cloves, peeled and minced
- 2 yellow onions, peeled and sliced
- 11 ounces celery, thinly sliced
- 1 tablespoon dried dill
- 3 bay leaves
- 4 cinnamon sticks, cut into halves
- Salt and pepper to taste

- 17 ounces of water

Directions

1. Take a bowl and add beef, add water and cover, let it soak for 2-3 hours
2. Drain and transfer to the Ninja Foodi
3. Add celery, onions, garlic, bay leaves, dill, cinnamon, dill, salt, pepper and rest of the water to the Ninja Foodi
4. Stir and combine it well
5. Lock lid and cook on HIGH pressure for 50 minutes
6. Release pressure naturally over 10 minutes
7. Transfer meat to cutting board and slice, divide amongst plates and pour the cooking liquid (alongside veggies) over the servings
8. Enjoy!

Nutrition Values (Per Serving)

Calories: 289
Fat: 21g
Carbohydrates: 14g
Protein: 9g

30. Hearty Korean Ribs

(Prepping time: 10 minutes\ Cooking time: 45 minutes |For 6 servings)

Ingredients

- 1 teaspoon olive oil
- 2 green onions, cut into 1-inch length
- 3 garlic cloves, smashed
- 3 quarter sized ginger slices
- 4 pounds beef short ribs, 3 inches thick, cut into 3 rib portions
- 1/2 cup of water
- 1/2 cup coconut aminos
- 1/4 cup dry white wine
- 2 teaspoons sesame oil
- Mince green onions for serving

Directions

1. Set your Ninja Foodi to "SAUTE" mode and add oil, let it shimmer
2. Add green onions, garlic, ginger, Saute for 1 minute
3. Add short ribs, water, amines, wine, sesame oil, and stir until the ribs are coated well

4. Lock lid and cook on HIGH pressure for 45 minutes
5. Release pressure naturally over 10 minutes
6. Remove short ribs from pot and serve with the cooking liquid
7. Enjoy!

Nutrition Values (Per Serving)

Calories: 423
Fat: 35g
Carbohydrates: 4g
Protein: 22g

31. Traditional Beef Sirloin Steak

(Prepping time: 5 minutes\ Cooking time: 17 minutes |For 4 servings)

Ingredients

- 3 tablespoons butter
- 1/2 teaspoon garlic powder
- 1-2 pounds beef sirloin steaks
- Salt and pepper to taste
- 1 garlic clove, minced

Directions

1. Set your Ninja Foodi to sauté mode and add butter, let the butter melt
2. Add beef sirloin steaks
3. Saute for 2 minutes on each side
4. Add garlic powder, garlic clove, salt, and pepper
5. Lock lid and cook on Medium-HIGH pressure for 15 minutes
6. Release pressure naturally over 10 minutes
7. Transfer prepare Steaks to a serving platter, enjoy!

Nutrition Values (Per Serving)

Calories: 246
Fat: 13g
Carbohydrates: 2g
Protein: 31g

32. Beef And Broccoli Platter

(Prepping time: 10 minutes\ Cooking time: 20 minutes |For 4 servings)

Ingredients

- 3 pounds beef chuck roast, cut into thin strips
- 1 tablespoon olive oil
- 1 yellow onion, peeled and chopped
- 1/2 cup beef stock
- 1 pound broccoli florets
- 2 teaspoons toasted sesame oil
- 2 tablespoons arrowroot

For Marinade

- 1 cup coconut aminos
- 1 tablespoon sesame oil
- 2 tablespoons fish sauce
- 5 garlic cloves, peeled and minced
- 3 red peppers, dried and crushed
- 1/2 teaspoon Chinese five spice powder
- Toasted sesame seeds, for serving

Directions

1. Take a bowl and mix in coconut aminos, fish sauce, 1 tablespoon sesame oil, garlic, five spice powder, crushed red pepper and stir
2. Add beef strips to the bowl and toss to coat
3. Keep it on the side for 10 minutes
4. Set your Ninja Foodi to "Saute" mode and add oil, let it heat up, add onion and stir cook for 4 minutes
5. Add beef and marinade, stir cook for 2 minutes
6. Add stock and stir
7. Lock the pressure lid of Ninja Foodi and cook on HIGH pressure for 5 minutes
8. Release pressure naturally over 10 minutes
9. Mix arrowroot with 1/4 cup liquid from the pot and gently pour the mixture back to the pot and stir
10. Place a steamer basket in the pot and add broccoli to the steamer rack, lock lid and cook on HIGH pressure for 3 minutes more, quick release pressure
11. Divide the dish between plates and serve with broccoli, toasted sesame seeds and enjoy!

Nutrition Values (Per Serving)

Calories: 433

Fat: 27g
Carbohydrates: 8g
Protein: 20g

33. Alternative Corned Cabbage And Beef

(Prepping time: 10 minutes\ Cooking time: 100 minutes |For 4 servings)

Ingredients

- 1 corned beef brisket
- 4 cups of water
- 1 small onion, peeled and quartered
- 3 garlic cloves, smashed and peeled
- 2 bay leaves
- 3 whole black peppercorns
- 1/2 teaspoon allspice berries
- 1 teaspoon dried thyme
- 5 medium carrots
- 1 cabbage, cut into wedges

Directions

1. Add corned beef, onion, garlic cloves, water, allspice, peppercorn, thymes to the Ninja Foodi
2. Lock up the lid and cook for about 90 minutes at HIGH pressure
3. Allow the pressure to release naturally once done
4. Open up and transfer the meat to your serving plate
5. Cover it with tin foil and allow it to cool for 15 minutes
6. Add carrots and cabbage to the lid and let them cook for 10 minutes at HIGH pressure
7. Once done, do a quick release. Take out the prepped veggies and serve with your corned beef

Nutrition Values (Per Serving)

Calories: 297
Fats: 17g
Carbs:1g
Protein: 14g

Chicken and Poultry Recipes

1. Crispy Roast Chicken

Serves: 6
Preparation time: 45 minutes

Ingredients:
- 1 whole chicken
- 2 tablespoons salt
- 1/4 cup lemon juice
- 1/4 cup honey
- 1/4 cup hot water
- 2 sprigs fresh thyme
- 5 cloves garlic
- 1 tablespoon vegetable oil

Preparation:
1. Season the chicken with the salt.
2. Pour the rest of the ingredients except the oil into the Ninja Foodi.
3. Place the chicken on the Ninja Foodi basket. Put the basket inside the pot.
4. Choose pressure function. Set it to high and cook for 15 minutes.
5. Release the pressure quickly. Brush the chicken with the vegetable oil.
6. Put on the crisping lid. Choose air crisp setting.
7. Cook at 400 degrees F for 15 minutes.

Serving Suggestion: Serve with steamed vegetables or fresh salad.

Tip: Add 5 more minutes to make the chicken crispier.

Nutritional Information Per Serving:
Calories 440
Total Fat 16.8g
Saturated Fat 4.5g
Cholesterol 173mg
Sodium 2496mg
Total Carbohydrate 12.9g
Dietary Fiber 0.2g
Total Sugars 11.9g

Protein 56.6g
Potassium 506mg

2. Ranch Chicken Wings

Serves: 4
Preparation time: 30 minutes

Ingredients:

- 1/2 cup water
- 2 tablespoons butter, melted
- 1-1/2 tablespoons apple cider vinegar
- 2 lb. frozen chicken wings
- 1/2 packet ranch salad dressing mix
- 1/2 teaspoon paprika
- Cooking spray

Preparation:

1. Pour the water, butter and vinegar into the pot. Mix well.
2. Put the chicken wings in the Ninja Foodi basket.
3. Cover and set it to pressure. Cook at high pressure for 5 minutes.
4. Release the pressure quickly. Season the chicken with the ranch and paprika.
5. Close the crisping lid. Set it to air crisp. Cook at 375 degrees F for 7 minutes.
6. Coat with the cooking spray and cook for 7 more minutes.

Serving Suggestion: Serve with ranch dip.

Tip: You can also use chili pepper flakes for spicy wings.

Nutritional Information Per Serving:

Calories 337
Total Fat 24.9g
Saturated Fat 8.8g
Cholesterol 84mg
Sodium 336mg
Total Carbohydrate 9.8g
Dietary Fiber 0.4g
Total Sugars 0.1g
Protein 17.4g

3. Chicken Parmesan

Serves: 4
Preparation time: 20 minutes

Ingredients:
- 2 chicken breasts, sliced into cutlets
- 6 tablespoons seasoned bread crumbs
- 2 tablespoons Parmesan cheese, grated
- 1 tablespoon butter, melted
- 6 tablespoons reduced fat mozzarella cheese
- 1/2 cup marinara sauce
- Cooking spray

Preparation:
1. Spray the Ninja Foodi basket with oil.
2. In a bowl, mix the bread crumbs and Parmesan cheese. In another bowl, place the butter. Coat the chicken with butter and dip into the bread crumb mix.
3. Place the cutlets on the basket. Seal the crisping lid. Set it to air crisp.
4. Cook at 375 degrees F for 6 minutes.
5. Flip and top with the marinara and mozzarella.

Serving Suggestion: Serve with pasta or salad.

Tip: Use whole wheat bread crumbs.

Nutritional Information Per Serving:
Calories 307
Total Fat 14.4g
Saturated Fat 6.5g
Cholesterol 87mg
Sodium 599mg
Total Carbohydrate 13.3g
Dietary Fiber 1.4g
Total Sugars 3.4g
Protein 30.8g
Potassium 303mg

4. Honey Chicken Wings

Serves: 2
Preparation time: 50 minutes

Ingredients:
- 1 lb. chicken wings
- 1/4 cup honey
- 2 tablespoons hot sauce
- 1-1/2 tablespoons soy sauce
- 1 tablespoon butter
- 1 tablespoon lime juice

Preparation:
1. Place the chicken wings in the Ninja Foodi basket. Add the basket to the pot.
2. Cover the crisping lid. Set it to air crisp. Cook at 360 degrees F for 30 minutes.
3. Flip every 10 minutes. Remove the wings and set aside. Set the pot to sauté.
4. Add the rest of the ingredients and mix well. Simmer for 3 minutes.
5. Toss the wings in the mixture before serving.

Serving Suggestion: Garnish with chopped chives.

Tip: Use freshly squeezed lime juice.

Nutritional Information Per Serving:
Calories 619
Total Fat 22.6g
Saturated Fat 8.3g
Cholesterol 217mg
Sodium 1295mg
Total Carbohydrate 36.1g
Dietary Fiber 0.2g
Total Sugars 35.2g
Protein 66.6g
Potassium 622mg

5. Chicken Nuggets

Serves: 4
Preparation time: 30 minutes

Ingredients:
- 2 teaspoons olive oil
- 6 tablespoons breadcrumbs
- 2 tablespoons grated parmesan cheese

- 2 chicken breasts, sliced into nuggets
- Salt and pepper to taste
- Cooking spray

Preparation:
1. Pour the olive oil in one bowl.
2. In another bowl, mix the bread crumbs and Parmesan.
3. Season the chicken with salt and pepper.
4. Coat with the olive oil and dip in the bread crumb mixture.
5. Place the chicken on the basket. Seal the crisping lid. Select the air crisp function.
6. Cook at 375 degrees F for 8 minutes.

Serving Suggestion: Serve with green salad or veggie sticks.

Tip: Use whole wheat bread crumbs.

Nutritional Information Per Serving:

Calories 245
Total Fat 11.4g
Saturated Fat 4g
Cholesterol 75mg
Sodium 267mg
Total Carbohydrate 7.8g
Dietary Fiber 0.5g
Total Sugars 0.6g
Protein 27g
Potassium 198mg

6. Peanut Chicken

Serves: 6
Preparation time: 30 minutes

Ingredients:

- 1-1/2 lb. chicken breast, sliced into cubes
- Salt to taste
- 1 teaspoon oil
- 3 clove garlic, chopped
- 1 tablespoon ginger, chopped
- 13 oz. coconut milk

- 3 tablespoons soy sauce
- 3 tablespoons honey
- 2 tablespoons fresh lime juice
- 1 tablespoon chili garlic paste
- 1/2 cup peanut butter

Preparation:

1. Season the chicken with salt. Set the Ninja Foodi to sauté. Add the oil.
2. Cook the garlic and ginger for 1 minute.
3. Add the chicken and all the other ingredients except the peanut butter.
4. Mix well. Put the peanut butter on top of the chicken but do not stir.
5. Seal the pot. Set it to pressure. Cook at high pressure for 9 minutes.
6. Release the pressure naturally.

Serving Suggestion: Serve on top of spinach leaves.

Tip: Spread peanut butter evenly on top of the chicken.

Nutritional Information Per Serving:

Calories 445
Total Fat 29.1g
Saturated Fat 15.4g
Cholesterol 73mg
Sodium 645mg
Total Carbohydrate 18g
Dietary Fiber 2.9g
Total Sugars 12.9g
Protein 31.5g
Potassium 762mg

7. Honey Teriyaki Chicken

Serves: 4
Preparation time: 50 minutes

Ingredients:

- 4 chicken breasts, sliced into strips
- 1 cup soy sauce
- 1/2 cup water
- 2/3 cup honey
- 2 teaspoons garlic, minced
- 1/2 cup rice vinegar
- 1/2 teaspoon ground ginger

- 1/4 teaspoon crushed red pepper flakes
- 3 tablespoons corn starch dissolved in 3 tablespoons cold water

Preparation:

1. Put the chicken inside the Ninja Foodi.
2. Add the rest of the ingredients except the corn starch mixture.
3. Put on the lid. Set it to pressure. Cook at high pressure for 30 minutes.
4. Release the pressure naturally. Set it to sauté.
5. Stir in the corn starch and simmer until the sauce has thickened.

Serving Suggestion: Garnish with sesame seeds and serve with fried rice.

Tip: Use low sodium soy sauce.

Nutritional Information Per Serving:

Calories 495
Total Fat 10.4g
Saturated Fat 2.9g
Cholesterol 125mg
Sodium 717mg
Total Carbohydrate 52.1g
Dietary Fiber 0.7g
Total Sugars 47.5g
Protein 44.8g
Potassium 519mg

8. Turkey & Broccoli

Serves: 4
Preparation time: 10 minutes

Ingredients:

- 2 tablespoons butter
- 2 lb. turkey breast, sliced into cubes
- 2 cloves garlic, crushed
- 1 onion, chopped
- Salt and pepper to taste
- 1 teaspoon garlic powder
- 1/2 cup milk
- 1 cup chicken stock
- 4 cups cooked rice
- 2 cups cooked broccoli

Preparation:

1. Set the Ninja Foodi to sauté. Add the butter. Cook the onion, garlic and turkey.
2. Brown both sides of turkey.
3. Add the rest of the ingredients except the rice and broccoli.
4. Cover the pot and set it to pressure. Cook at high pressure for 5 minutes.
5. Release the pressure quickly. Serve with the broccoli and rice.

Serving Suggestion: Serve with long grain white rice.

Tip: You can also pair this with other vegetables such as carrots or potatoes.

Nutritional Information Per Serving:

Calories 459
Total Fat 17g
Saturated Fat 10g
Cholesterol 48mg
Sodium 1121mg
Total Carbohydrates 61g
Dietary Fiber 2g
Sugars 3g
Protein 14g 28%
Potassium 322mg

9. Garlic Paprika Turkey Thighs

Serves: 4
Preparation time: 30 minutes

Ingredients:

- 2 lb. turkey thighs
- 2 teaspoons smoked paprika
- Salt and pepper to taste
- 3 tablespoons butter, divided
- 4 cloves garlic, minced
- 1 cup chicken stock
- 1/2 cup heavy cream
- 1 tablespoon corn starch
- 1/2 cup Parmesan cheese, grated

Preparation:

1. Season the turkey with salt and pepper. Choose sauté function in the Ninja Foodi.
2. Add the butter. Cook the turkey until brown on both sides.
3. Remove and set aside. Add the garlic and cook for 30 seconds.
4. Stir in the chicken stock. Put the turkey back to the pot.
5. Seal the pot. Set it to pressure. Cook at high pressure for 7 minutes.
6. Release the pressure quickly. Press sauté function.
7. Stir in the heavy cream and corn starch. Sprinkle Parmesan cheese on top.

Serving Suggestion: Garnish with fresh parsley.

Tip: Use freshly grated Parmesan cheese.

Nutritional Information Per Serving:

Calories 405
Total Fat 28.7g
Saturated Fat 13.6g
Cholesterol 143mg
Sodium 977mg
Total Carbohydrate 4.6g
Dietary Fiber 0.5g
Total Sugars 0.4g
Protein 31.6g
Potassium 433mg

10. Chicken Carnitas

Serves: 6
Preparation time: 30 minutes

Ingredients:

- Salt and pepper to taste
- 1 tablespoon oregano
- 1 tablespoon cumin
- 1 teaspoon chili powder
- 1 tablespoon olive oil
- 1 onion, chopped
- 4 cloves garlic, minced
- 1/4 cup orange juice
- 1/4 cup lime juice
- 1/4 cup chicken stock

- 1 lb. chicken breast
- Cooking spray

Preparation:

1. In a bowl, combine the salt, pepper, oregano, cumin and chili powder.
2. Pour in the olive oil to the Ninja Foodi. Choose the sauté function. Add the onion.
3. Cook until translucent. Add the garlic and cook for 1 minute.
4. Add the rest of the ingredients including the spice blend.
5. Mix well. Seal the pot. Set it to pressure. Cook at high pressure for 8 minutes.
6. Release the pressure quickly. Spray the chicken with oil. Transfer to the basket.
7. Set the pot to air crisp. Seal the crisping lid. Cook for 5 minutes.

Serving Suggestion: Garnish with fresh cilantro.

Tip: Use low sodium chicken stock.

Nutritional Information Per Serving:

Calories 134
Total Fat 4g
Cholesterol 48mg
Sodium 487mg
Total Carbohydrates 6g
Dietary Fiber 1g
Sugars 2g
Protein 16g
Potassium 382mg

11. Lemon Chicken with Garlic

Serves: 6
Preparation time: 20 minutes

Ingredients:

- 6 chicken thighs
- Salt and pepper to taste
- 1/2 teaspoon red chili flakes
- 1/2 teaspoon garlic powder
- 1/2 teaspoon smoked paprika
- 2 tablespoons olive oil
- 3 tablespoons butter

- 1 onion, chopped
- 4 cloves garlic, minced
- 1 tablespoon lemon juice
- 1/4 cup low sodium broth
- 2 teaspoons Italian seasoning
- Lemon zest
- 2 tablespoons heavy cream

Preparation:

1. Sprinkle the chicken thighs with salt, pepper, chili flakes, garlic powder and paprika.
2. Set the Ninja Foodi to sauté. Add the olive oil.
3. Cook the chicken for 3 minutes per side. Remove from the pot and set aside.
4. Melt the butter in the pot. Add the onion and garlic. Deglaze the pot with the lemon juice. Cook for 1 minute. Add the chicken broth, seasoning and lemon zest.
5. Set the pot to pressure. Seal it. Cook at high pressure for 7 minutes.
6. Release the pressure naturally. Stir in the heavy cream before serving.

Serving Suggestion: Garnish with fresh parsley.

Tip: You can also use chicken breasts and slice horizontally.

Nutritional Information Per Serving:

Calories 403
Total Fat 23.6g
Saturated Fat 8.5g
Cholesterol 153mg
Sodium 171mg
Total Carbohydrate 3g
Dietary Fiber 0.5g
Total Sugars 1.1g
Protein 42.8g
Potassium 406mg

12. Chicken Cacciatore

Serves: 4
Preparation time: 50 minutes

Ingredients:

- 4 chicken thighs

- 2 tablespoons olive oil
- 1/2 onion, chopped
- 2 cloves garlic, minced
- 3 stalks celery, chopped
- 4 oz. mushrooms
- 14 oz. stewed tomatoes
- 2 teaspoons herbes de Provence
- 3/4 cup water
- 3 cubes chicken bouillon, crumbled
- 2 tablespoons tomato paste

Preparation:

1. Set the Ninja Foodi to sauté. Add the oil and chicken.
2. Cook the chicken for 6 minutes per side. Remove the chicken and set aside.
3. Add the onion, garlic, celery and mushrooms. Cook for 5 minutes, stirring frequently.
4. Put the chicken back. Pour in the tomatoes and tomato paste.
5. Add the rest of the ingredients. Seal the pot.
6. Set it to pressure. Cook at high pressure for 15 minutes. Release the pressure quickly.

Serving Suggestion: Serve with pasta or rice.

Tip: Add red pepper flakes if you like the dish spicy.

Nutritional Information Per Serving:

Calories 383
Total Fat 18.5g
Saturated Fat 4.3g
Cholesterol 130mg
Sodium 153mg
Total Carbohydrate 8.9g
Dietary Fiber 2.7g
Total Sugars 5.2g
Protein 45.1g
Potassium 821mg

13. Chicken Marsala

Serves: 4
Preparation time: 40 minutes

Ingredients:

- 4 chicken breasts, sliced into strips
- 1 teaspoon garlic powder
- Salt and pepper to taste
- 1/2 cup all purpose flour
- 3 tablespoons butter
- 3 tablespoons olive oil
- 3 cloves garlic, minced
- 1 shallot, sliced thinly
- 8 oz. mushrooms
- 2/3 cup Marsala wine
- 2/3 cup chicken stock
- 1/2 cup heavy cream

Preparation:

1. Season the chicken with garlic powder, salt and pepper. Coat the chicken with flour.
2. Place the chicken on the Ninja Foodi basket. Put the basket inside the pot.
3. Seal the crisping lid. Set it to air crisp. Cook at 375 degrees F for 15 minutes.
4. Remove and set aside. Set the pot to sauté. Add the butter and oil.
5. Cook the garlic, shallot and mushrooms. Pour in the wine and chicken broth.
6. Simmer for 10 minutes. Stir in the heavy cream.
7. Toss the chicken into the mixture. Serve.

Serving Suggestion: Garnish with chopped parsley.

Tip: Use whole wheat flour.

Nutritional Information Per Serving:

Calories 622
Total Fat 35g
Saturated Fat 14g
Cholesterol 173mg
Sodium 349mg
Total Carbohydrates 23g
Dietary Fiber 1g
Sugars 5g
Protein 41g
Potassium 966mg

14. Barbecue Chicken

Serves: 8
Preparation time: 20 minutes

Ingredients:

- 1 tablespoon olive oil
- 3 chicken breasts (boneless and skinless)
- 1 teaspoon garlic powder
- Salt and pepper to taste
- 1 cup barbecue sauce
- 1/2 cup water

Preparation:

1. Pour the olive oil into the Ninja Foodi. Add the rest of the ingredients. Mix well.
2. Pour the barbecue sauce over the chicken. Do not stir. Seal the pot.
3. Set it to pressure. Cook at high pressure for 10 minutes.
4. Release the pressure naturally. Shred the chicken meat and toss in barbecue sauce.

Serving Suggestion: Serve with steamed vegetables.

Tip: Use low sodium barbecue sauce.

Nutritional Information Per Serving:

Calories 167
Total Fat 5.9g
Saturated Fat 1.4g
Cholesterol 49mg
Sodium 397mg
Total Carbohydrate 11.6g
Dietary Fiber 0.2g
Total Sugars 8.2g
Protein 15.9g
Potassium 202mg

15. Chicken Chile Verde

Serves: 6
Preparation time: 30 minutes

Ingredients:

- 2 lb. chicken thighs
- 1/4 teaspoon garlic powder
- 16 ounces salsa verde
- 1/2 teaspoon ground cumin
- Salt and pepper to taste

Preparation:

1. Add the chicken to the Ninja Foodi.
2. Season with the garlic powder, salsa verde and cumin. Cover the pot.
3. Set it to pressure. Cook at high pressure for 25 minutes.
4. Release the pressure quickly. Shred the chicken using 2 forks.
5. Season with the salt and pepper.

Serving Suggestion: Serve with whole wheat tortillas.

Tip: Shredded chicken can be stored for up to 3 days in the refrigerator.

Nutritional Information Per Serving:

Calories 307
Total Fat 11.4g
Saturated Fat 3.1g
Cholesterol 135mg
Sodium 564mg
Total Carbohydrate 3.4g
Dietary Fiber 0.3g
Total Sugars 1.2g
Protein 44.8g
Potassium 372mg

16. Lemon And Chicken Extravaganza

(Prepping time: 5 minutes\ Cooking time: 18 minutes |For 4 servings)

Ingredients

- 4 bone-in, skin on chicken thighs
- Salt and pepper to taste
- 2 tablespoons butter, divided
- 2 teaspoons garlic, minced
- 1/2 cup herbed chicken stock
- 1/2 cup heavy whip cream
- 1/2 a lemon, juiced

Directions

1. Season your chicken thighs generously with salt and pepper
2. Set your Foodi to sauté mode and add oil, let it heat up
3. Add thigh, Sauté both sides for 6 minutes. Remove thigh to a platter and keep it on the side
4. Add garlic, cook for 2 minutes. Whisk in chicken stock, heavy cream, lemon juice and gently stir
5. Bring the mix to a simmer and reintroduce chicken
6. Lock lid and cook for 10 minutes on HIGH pressure
7. Release pressure over 10 minutes. Serve and enjoy!

Nutrition Values (Per Serving)

Calories: 294
Fat: 26g
Carbohydrates: 4g
Protein: 12g

17. Bruschetta Chicken Meal

(Prepping time: 5 minutes\ Cooking time: 9 minutes |For 4 servings)

Ingredients

- 2 tablespoons balsamic vinegar
- 1/3 cup olive oil
- 2 teaspoons garlic cloves, minced
- 1 teaspoon black pepper
- 1/2 teaspoon salt
- 1/2 cup sun-dried tomatoes, in olive oil
- 2 pounds chicken breasts, quartered, boneless
- 2 tablespoons fresh basil, chopped

Direction

1. Take a bowl and whisk in vinegar, oil, garlic, pepper, salt
2. Fold in tomatoes, basil and add breast, mix well. Transfer to fridge and let it sit for 30 minutes
3. Add everything to Ninja Foodi and lock lid, cook on High Pressure for 9 minutes
4. Quick release pressure. Serve and enjoy!

Nutrition Values (Per Serving)

Calories: 480

Fat: 26g
Carbohydrates: 4g
Protein: 52g

18. The Great Hainanese Chicken

(Prepping time: 20 minutes \ Cooking time: 4 hours |For 4 servings)

Ingredients

- 1 ounces ginger, peeled
- 6 garlic cloves, crushed
- 6 bundles cilantro/basil leaves
- 1 teaspoon salt
- 1 tablespoon sesame oil
- 3 (1 and 1/2 pounds each) chicken meat, ready to cook

For Dip

- 2 tablespoons ginger, minced
- 1 teaspoon garlic, minced
- 1 tablespoon chicken stock
- 1 teaspoon sesame oil
- 1/2 teaspoon sugar
- Salt to taste

Directions

1. Add chicken, garlic, ginger, leaves, and salt in your Ninja Food
2. Add enough water to fully submerge chicken, lock lid cook on SLOW COOK mode on LOW for 4 hours. Release pressure naturally
3. Take chicken out of pot and chill for 10 minutes
4. Take a bowl and add all the dipping ingredients and blend well in a food processor
5. Take chicken out of ice bath and drain, chop into serving pieces. Arrange onto a serving platter
6. Brush chicken with sesame oil. Serve with ginger dip. Enjoy!

Nutrition Values (Per Serving)

Calories: 535
Fat: 45g
Carbohydrates: 5g
Protein: 28g

19. A Genuine Hassel Back Chicken

(Prepping time: 5 minutes\ Cooking time: 60 minutes |For 4 servings)

Ingredients

- 4 tablespoons butter
- Salt and pepper to taste
- 2 cups fresh mozzarella cheese, thinly sliced
- 8 large chicken breasts
- 4 large Roma tomatoes, thinly sliced

Directions

1. Make few deep slits in chicken breasts, season with salt and pepper
2. Stuff mozzarella cheese slices and tomatoes in chicken slits
3. Grease Ninja Foodi pot with butter and arrange stuffed chicken breasts
4. Lock lid and BAKE/ROAST for 1 hour at 365 degrees F. Serve and enjoy!

Nutrition Values (Per Serving)

Calories: 278
Fat: 15g
Carbohydrates: 3.8g
Protein: 15g

20. Shredded Up Salsa Chicken

(Prepping time: 5 minutes\ Cooking time: 20 minutes |For 4 servings)

Ingredients

- 1 pound chicken breast, skin and bones removed
- 3/4 teaspoon cumin
- 1/2 teaspoon salt
- Pinch of oregano
- Pepper to taste
- 1 cup chunky salsa Keto friendly

Directions

1. Season chicken with spices and add to Ninja Foodi
2. Cover with salsa and lock lid, cook on HIGH pressure for 20 minutes
3. Quick release pressure. Add chicken to a platter and shred the chicken. Serve and enjoy!

Nutrition Values (Per Serving)

Calories: 125
Fat: 3g
Carbohydrates: 2g
Protein: 22g

21. Mexico's Favorite Chicken Soup

(Prepping time: 5 minutes\ Cooking time: 20 minutes |For 4 servings)

Ingredients

- 2 cups chicken, shredded
- 4 tablespoons olive oil
- 1/2 cup cilantro, chopped
- 8 cups chicken broth
- 1/3 cup salsa
- 1 teaspoon onion powder
- 1/2 cup scallions, chopped
- 4 ounces green chilies, chopped
- 1/2 teaspoon habanero, minced
- 1 cup celery root, chopped
- 1 teaspoon cumin
- 1 teaspoon garlic powder
- Salt and pepper to taste

Directions

1. Add all ingredients to Ninja Foodi. Stir and lock lid, cook on HIGH pressure for 10 minutes
2. Release pressure naturally over 10 minutes. Serve and enjoy!

Nutrition Values (Per Serving)

Calories: 204
Fat: 14g
Carbohydrates: 4g
Protein: 14g

22. Taiwanese Chicken Delight

(Prepping time: 5 minutes\ Cooking time: 10 minutes |For 4 servings)

Ingredients

- 6 dried red chilis
- 1/4 cup sesame oil
- 2 tablespoons ginger
- 1/4 cup garlic, minced
- 1/4 cup red wine vinegar
- 1/4 cup coconut aminos
- Salt as needed
- 1.2 teaspoon xanthan gum (for the finish)
- 1/4 cup Thai basil, chopped

Directions

1. Set your Ninja Foodi to Saute mode and add ginger, chilis, garlic and Saute for 2 minutes
2. Add remaining ingredients. Lock lid and cook on HIGH pressure for 10 minutes
3. Quick release pressure. Serve and enjoy!

Nutrition Values (Per Serving)

Calories: 307
Fat: 15g
Carbohydrates: 7g
Protein: 31g

23. Cabbage And Chicken Meatballs

(Prepping time: 10 minutes + 30 minutes\ Cooking time: 4-6 minutes |For 4 servings)

Ingredients

- 1 pound ground chicken
- 1/4 cup heavy whip cream
- 2 teaspoons salt
- 1/2 teaspoon ground caraway seeds
- 1 and 1/2 teaspoons fresh ground black pepper, divided
- 1/4 teaspoon ground allspice
- 4-6 cups green cabbage, thickly chopped
- 1/2 cup almond milk
- 2 tablespoons unsalted butter

Directions

1. Transfer meat to a bowl and add cream, 1 teaspoon salt, caraway, ½ teaspoon pepper, allspice and mix it well. Let the mixture chill for 30 minutes
2. Once the mixture is ready, use your hands to scoop the mixture into meatballs
3. Add half of your balls to Ninja Foodi pot and cover with half of the cabbage
4. Add remaining balls and cover with rest of the cabbage
5. Add milk, pats of butter, season with salt and pepper
6. Lock lid and cook on HIGH pressure for 4 minutes. Quick release pressure
7. Unlock lid and serve. Enjoy!

Nutrition Values (Per Serving)

Calories: 294
Fat: 26g
Carbohydrates: 4g
Protein: 12g

24. Poached Chicken With Coconut Lime Cream Sauce

(Prepping time: 5 minutes \ Cooking time: 10 minutes |For 4 servings)

Ingredients

- 1-ounce shallot, minced
- 1 ounces ginger, sliced
- 2 medium banana peppers,
- 1 cup of coconut milk
- 1 cup chicken stock
- Juice of 1 lime, and zest
- 2 tablespoons fish sauce
- 3 pieces of 1/3 pounds each chicken breasts, meat

Directions

1. Add listed ingredients to your Ninja Foodi
2. Stir well and lock lid, cook on HIGH pressure for 10 minutes
3. Quick release pressure. Top with fresh cilantro. Serve and enjoy!

Nutrition Values (Per Serving)

Calories: 425
Fat: 33g
Carbohydrates: 9g

Protein: 24g

25. Hot And Spicy Paprika Chicken

(Prepping time: 10 minutes\ Cooking time: 20-25 minutes |For 4 servings)

Ingredients

- 4 piece (4 ounces each) chicken breast, skin on
- Salt and pepper to taste
- 1/2 cup sweet onion, chopped
- 1/2 cup heavy whip cream
- 2 teaspoons smoked paprika
- 1/2 cup sour cream
- 2 tablespoons fresh parsley, chopped

Directions

1. Season chicken with salt and pepper
2. Set your Foodi to Saute mode and add oil, let it heat up
3. Add chicken and sear both sides until nicely browned. Should take around 15 minutes
4. Remove chicken and transfer to a plate
5. Take a skillet and place it over medium heat, add onion and Sauté for 4 minutes
6. Stir in cream, paprika, bring the liquid to simmer. Return chicken to skillet and warm
7. Transfer the whole mixture to your Foodi and lock lid, cook on HIGH pressure for 5 minutes
8. Release pressure naturally over 10 minutes. Stir in cream, serve and enjoy!

Nutrition Values (Per Serving)

Calories: 389
Fat: 30g
Carbohydrates: 4g
Protein: 25g

26. Inspiring Turkey Cutlets

(Prepping time: 10 minutes\ Cooking time: 20-25 minutes |For 4 servings)

Ingredients

- 1 teaspoon Greek seasoning
- 1 pound turkey cutlets

- 2 tablespoons olive oil
- 1 teaspoon turmeric powder
- 1/2 cup almond flour

Directions

1. Take a bowl and add Greek seasoning, turmeric powder, almond flour, and mix
2. Dredge turkey cutlets in a bowl and let them sit for 30 minutes
3. Set Ninja Foodi to Sauté mode and add oil, let it heat up. Add cutlets and Sauté for 2 minutes
4. Lock lid and cook on LOW- MEDIUM pressure for 20 minutes
5. Release pressure naturally over 10 minutes. Take it out and serve, enjoy!

Nutrition Values (Per Serving)

Calories: 340
Fat: 19g
Carbohydrates: 4g
Protein: 36g

27. Lemongrass And Tamarind Chicken

(Prepping time: 10 minutes \ Cooking time: 4 hours |For 4 servings)

Ingredients

- 3 chicken thighs
- 1 ounce strips fresh turmeric
- 2 shallots, quartered
- Handful of mustard
- 1 stalk lemongrass, bruised and bundled up
- 2 cups chicken stock
- 1 banana pepper
- 4 tablespoons olive oil
- 2 tablespoons tamarind paste
- 2 Roma tomatoes, quartered
- 1 radish, peeled and chopped
- Fish sauce to taste
- Salt and pepper to taste

Directions

1. Add listed ingredients to your Ninja Foodi
2. Stir well and lock lid, cook on HIGH pressure for 10 minutes

3. Quick release pressure. Top with fresh cilantro. Serve and enjoy!

Nutrition Values (Per Serving)

Calories: 445
Fat: 32g
Carbohydrates: 28g
Protein: 28g

28. Fluffy Whole Chicken Dish

(Prepping time: 10 minutes\ Cooking time: 8 hours |For 4 servings)

Ingredients

- 1 cup mozzarella cheese
- 4 whole garlic cloves, peeled
- 1 whole chicken (2 pounds), cleaned and pat dried
- Salt and pepper to taste
- 2 tablespoons fresh lemon juice

Directions

1. Stuff chicken cavity with garlic cloves and mozzarella cheese
2. Season chicken generously with salt and pepper
3. Transfer chicken to Ninja Foodi and drizzle lemon juice
4. Lock lid and set to Slow Cooker mode, let it cook on LOW for 8 hours
5. Once done, serve and enjoy!

Nutrition Values (Per Serving)

Calories: 309
Fat: 12g
Carbohydrates: 1.6g
Protein: 45g

29. Sensible Chettinad Chicken

(Prepping time: 10 minutes\ Cooking time: 15 minutes |For 4 servings)

Ingredients

- 1 pound of boneless chicken thigh cut up into pieces
- 1 tablespoon of Ghee
- 1 bay leaf
- 5 curry leaves
- 1 inch Ginger piece

- 5 cloves of Garlic
- 1/4 cup of grated coconut (fresh)
- 1 large onion, diced
- 2 medium tomatoes, diced
- 1 teaspoon of salt
- 1/2 a cup of water
- Cilantro as needed

Whole Spices

- 4 pieces of Red Chili Whole Kashmiri
- 1 teaspoon of black peppercorns
- 1 teaspoon of cumin seeds
- 2 teaspoon of coriander seeds
- 5 pieces of Green coriander
- 1 stick of cinnamon
- 4 pieces of cloves
- 1 tablespoon of cloves
- 1 tablespoon of poppy seeds
- 1 teaspoon of fennel seeds

Directions

1. Set your Ninja Foodi to Saute mode and add whole spices and cook them until dry roasted (for about 30 seconds)
2. Add garlic, ginger, grated coconut and Saute for 30 seconds more
3. Transfer the mixture to a blender and Grind until you have a paste. This is your Chettinad Spice Mix. Clean the Ninja Foodi and set your pot to Saute mode again
4. Add oil and allow it to heat it up. Add bay leaf and curry leaves, Saute for 30 seconds
5. Add diced up onions and Saute for about 30 seconds
6. Add diced up onion and Saute for 3 minutes
7. Add tomatoes, salt and ground spices and Saute for 2 minutes (including the previous blend)
8. Add chicken pieces and Saute for 3 minutes more
9. Add water and lock up the lid, cook for 5 minutes at HIGH pressure
10. Once done, do a quick release and enjoy with a garnish of cilantro. Enjoy!

Nutrition Values (Per Serving)

Calories: 198
Fat: 6g
Carbohydrates: 8g

Protein: 28g

30. Hawaiian Pinna Colada Chicken Meal

(Prepping time: 10 minutes\ Cooking time: 15 minutes |For 4 servings)

Ingredients

- 2 pounds organic chicken thigh
- 1 cup fresh pineapple chunks
- 1/2 cup coconut cream
- 1 teaspoon cinnamon
- 1/8 teaspoon salt
- 2 tablespoons coconut aminos
- 1/2 cup green onion, chopped
- Arrowroot flout

Directions

1. Add all of the ingredients to your Ninja Foodi except green onion
2. Lock up the lid and cook for 15 minutes at HIGH pressure
3. Once done, allow the pressure to release naturally. Open up the lid and stir well
4. Take a bowl and mix arrowroot flour and a tablespoon of water to make a slurry
5. Add the slurry to your pot and mix well to make a thick mixture
6. Set your pot to Saute mode and wait until the sauce is just thick enough
7. Garnish with some green onion and enjoy!

Nutrition Values (Per Serving)

Calories: 358
Fat: 20g
Carbohydrates: 8g
Protein: 12g

31. Garlic and Butter Chicken Dish

(Prepping time: 10 minutes\ Cooking time: 35 minutes |For 4 servings)

Ingredients

- 4 pieces of chicken breasts, chopped up
- 1/4 cup of turmeric ghee/ normal ghee
- 1 teaspoon of salt
- 10 cloves of garlic, peeled and diced up

Directions

1. Add chicken breast to the Ninja Foodi
2. Add ghee, salt, diced garlic and lock up the lid
3. Cook on HIGH pressure for 35 minutes
4. Release the pressure naturally and open the lid
5. Serve with extra ghee

Nutrition Values (Per Serving)

Protein: 47g
Carbs: 3g
Fats: 21g
Calories: 404

32. Creamy Chicken Curry

(Prepping time: 10 minutes\ Cooking time: 10 hours |For 4 servings)

Ingredients

- 10 bone-in chicken thighs, skinless
- 1 cup sour cream
- 2 tablespoons. Curry powder
- 1 onion, chopped
- 1 jar (16 ounces) chunky salsa sauce

Directions

1. Add chicken thigh to your Ninja Foodi
2. Add onions, salsa, curry powder over chicken, stir and place the lid
3. Cook SLOW COOK MODE (LOW) for 10 hours. Open lid and transfer chicken to a serving platter
4. Pour sour cream into the sauce (cooking liquid) in the Ninja Foodi
5. Stir well and pour the sauce over chicken. Serve!

Nutrition Values (Per Serving)

Calories: 400
Fat: 20g
Carbohydrates: 17g
Protein: 39g

33. Lemon And Artichoke Medley

(Prepping time: 10 minutes\ Cooking time: 8 hours |For 6 servings)

Ingredients

- 1 pound boneless and skinless chicken breast
- 1 pound boneless and skinless chicken thigh
- 14 ounces (can) artichoke hearts, packed in water and drained
- 1 onion, diced
- 2 carrots, diced
- 3 garlic cloves, minced
- 1 bay leaf
- 1/2 teaspoon pepper
- 3 cups turnips, peeled and cubed
- 6 cups chicken broth
- 14 cup fresh lemon juice
- 1/4 cup parsley, chopped

Directions

1. Add the above mentioned ingredients to your Ninja Foodi except for lemon juice and parsley
2. Cook on Slow Cooker (LOW) for 8 hours. Remove the chicken and shred it up
3. Return it back to the Ninja Foodi. Season with some pepper and salt!
4. Stir in parsley and lemon juice and serve!

Nutrition Values (Per Serving)

Calories: 400
Fat: 10g
Carbohydrates: 12g
Protein: 3g

34. Awesome Sesame Ginger Chicken

(Prepping time: 10 minutes\ Cooking time: 10 minutes |For 4 servings)

Ingredients

- 1 tablespoon rice vinegar
- 1 tablespoon Truvia
- 1 tablespoon garlic, minced
- 1 tablespoon fresh ginger, minced
- 1 tablespoon sesame oil
- 2 tablespoons soy sauce
- 1 and 1/2 pound boneless, skinless chicken thigh, cut into large pieces

Directions

1. Take a heatproof bowl and add soy sauce, ginger, sesame oil, garlic, Truvia and vinegar
2. Stir well to coat it. Cover bowl with foil. Add 2 cups of water to Ninja Foodie's inner pot
3. Place a trivet and place the bowl with chicken on the trivet
4. Lock lid and cook for 10 minutes on HIGH pressure. Release pressure naturally over 10 minutes
5. Remove chicken and shred it, mix it back into the bowl. Serve and enjoy!

Nutrition Values (Per Serving)

Calories: 118, Fats: 10g, Carbs: 7g ,Protein: 3g

35. Chicken Korma

(Prepping time: 10 minutes\ Cooking time: 20 minutes |For 6 servings)

Ingredients

1 pound of chicken

For Sauce

- 1 ounce of cashews
- 1 small chopped onion
- 1/2 a cup of diced tomatoes
- 1/2 of green Serrano pepper
- 5 cloves of garlic
- 1 teaspoon of minced ginger
- 1 teaspoon of turmeric
- 1 teaspoon of Garam masala
- 1 teaspoon of cumin-coriander powder
- 1/2 a teaspoon of cayenne pepper
- 1/2 a cup of water

For topping

1 teaspoon of Garam masala
1/2 a cup of coconut milk
1/4 cup of chopped cilantro

Directions

1. Add the sauce ingredients to a blender and blend them well
2. Pour the sauce to your Ninja Foodi. Place the chicken on top

3. Lock up the lid and cook on HIGH pressure for 10 minutes
4. Release the pressure naturally. Take the chicken out and cut into bite-sized portions
5. Add coconut milk, Garam masala to the pot
6. Transfer the chicken back and garnish with cilantro. Enjoy!

Nutrition Values (Per Serving)

Calories: 388, Fats: 14g, Carbs: 16g, Protein: 48g

36. Turkey With Garlic Sauce

(Prepping time: 10 minutes\ Cooking time: 8 hours |For 6 servings)

Ingredients

- 5 large onions, thinly sliced
- 4 garlic cloves, minced
- 1/4 cup white wine vinegar
- 1/2 teaspoon salt
- 1/4 teaspoon ground black pepper
- 1/4 teaspoon cayenne pepper
- 4 large skinless turkey thighs

Directions

1. Gently lay the garlic and onions into the bottom of your Ninja Foodi
2. Pour in some wine with a sprinkle of salt, cayenne pepper, and black pepper.
3. Add turkey thighs and cover it up. Let it cook SLOW COOKER MODE (low) for about 8 hours.
4. Remove the turkey from the crock pot and clean up the flesh from the bones.
5. Keep the lid open and keep cooking until the liquid has completely evaporated, making sure to stir from time to time. Return the turkey to the pot.
6. Nestle the turkey into the mix. Serve hot. Enjoy!

Nutrition Values (Per Serving)

Calories: 845, Fat: 41g, Carbohydrates: 7g, Protein: 45g

Fish and Seafood Recipes

1. Fish & Fries

Serves: 4
Preparation time: 30 minutes

Ingredients:

- 1 lb. potatoes, sliced into strips
- 2 tablespoons olive oil
- Salt and pepper to taste
- 1/4 cup all purpose flour
- 1 egg
- 2 tablespoons water
- 2/3 cup cornflakes, crushed
- 1 tablespoon Parmesan cheese, grated
- 1 lb. cod fillets

Preparation:

1. Coat the potato strips with oil, salt and pepper. Place in the Ninja Foodi basket.
2. Seal the crisping lid and set it to air crisp.
3. Cook at 400 degrees F for 10 minutes, stirring halfway through.
4. While waiting, combine the flour with salt and pepper in one bowl.
5. In another bowl, beat the egg and add water.
6. In the third bowl, mix the cornflakes and Parmesan.
7. Dip each fillet in the flour mixture. Then dip into the second and third bowls.
8. Place in the Ninja Foodi basket. Seal the lid and choose air crisp function.
9. Cook at 400 degrees for 10 minutes.

Serving Suggestion: Serve with tartar sauce.

Tip: Sprinkle with salt and pepper before serving.

Nutritional Information Per Serving:

Calories 312
Total Fat 10.8g
Saturated Fat 2.4g

Cholesterol 101mg
Sodium 191mg
Total Carbohydrate 28.1g
Dietary Fiber 3.1g
Total Sugars 1.9g
Protein 26.7g
Potassium 493mg

2. Ranch Fish Fillet

Serves: 4
Preparation time: 20 minutes

Ingredients:

- 3/4 cup bread crumbs
- 1 packet dry ranch dressing mix
- 2 1/2 tablespoons vegetable oil
- 2 eggs, beaten
- 4 fish fillets

Preparation:

1. Combine the bread crumbs and ranch mix in a bowl. Pour in the oil.
2. Dip each fish fillet into the egg and cover with the crumb mixture.
3. Place in the Ninja Foodi basket. Seal the lid. Select air crisp function.
4. Cook at 360 degrees F for 12 minutes, flipping halfway through.

Serving Suggestion: Garnish with lemon wedges.

Tip: For added flavor, season the fish with salt and pepper.

Nutritional Information Per Serving:

Calories 425
Total Fat 25.4g
Saturated Fat 5.7g
Cholesterol 113mg
Sodium 697mg
Total Carbohydrate 30.4g
Dietary Fiber 1.4g
Total Sugars 1.4g
Protein 18.8g
Potassium 360mg

3. Paprika Salmon

Serves: 2
Preparation time: 15 minutes

Ingredients:

- 2 salmon fillets
- 2 teaspoons avocado oil
- 2 teaspoons paprika
- Salt and pepper to taste

Preparation:

1. Coat the salmon with oil. Season with salt, pepper and paprika.
2. Place in the Ninja Foodi basket. Set it to air crisp function.
3. Seal the crisping lid. Cook at 390 degrees for 7 minutes.

Serving Suggestion: Garnish with lemon slices.

Tip: Cooking depends on the fish fillet thickness. You may need to cook longer for thicker cuts.

Nutritional Information Per Serving:

Calories 248
Total Fat 11.9g
Cholesterol 78mg
Sodium 79mg
Total Carbohydrate 1.5g
Dietary Fiber 1g
Total Sugars 0.2g
Protein 34.9g
Potassium 748mg

4. Fish & Chips with Herb Sauce

Serves: 4
Preparation time: 50 minutes

Ingredients:

- 2 potatoes, sliced into strips
- Salt to taste
- 1/4 cup flour
- 1 egg
- 1 teaspoon Dijon mustard

- 3/4 cup seasoned panko bread crumbs
- 2 1/2 teaspoons olive oil
- 4 cod fish fillets

For the sauce:

- 1/4 cup light mayonnaise
- 2 tablespoons sour cream
- 2 tablespoons dill pickle, chopped
- 2 tablespoons red onion, chopped
- 1 tablespoon dill, chopped
- 1 tablespoon tarragon, chopped
- 2 teaspoons capers

Preparation:

1. Soak the potato strips in a bowl of water for 30 minutes.
2. Drain the water and pat the potatoes dry using a paper towel.
3. Place the potato strips in the Ninja Foodi basket.
4. Seal the crisping lid and choose air crisp function.
5. Cook at 360 degrees for 25 minutes, turning once or twice.
6. Season with the salt. Put the flour in a bowl.
7. Beat the egg and add the mustard in another bowl.
8. Mix the oil and bread crumbs on a shallow plate.
9. Coat the fish with the flour then the egg mixture, and then the oil with crumbs. Place in the basket. Cook at 360 degrees for 10 minutes.
10. Mix all the ingredients for the sauce and serve with the fish and fries.

Serving Suggestion: Garnish with cucumber and tomato slices.

Tip: Add cayenne pepper to make the sauce spicy.

Nutritional Information Per Serving:

Calories 409
Total Fat 12.1g
Saturated Fat 2.6g
Cholesterol 146mg
Sodium 426mg
Total Carbohydrate 27.9g
Dietary Fiber 3.2g
Total Sugars 2.6g
Protein 45.8g
Potassium 956mg

5. Southern Fried Fish Fillet

Serves: 4
Preparation time: 30 minutes

Ingredients:
- 2 lb. white fish fillet
- 1 cup low fat milk
- 1 lemon slice
- 1/2 cup mustard
- 1/2 cup cornmeal
- 1/4 cup all purpose flour
- 2 tablespoons dried parsley flakes
- Salt and pepper to taste
- 1/4 teaspoon chili powder
- 1/4 teaspoon garlic powder
- 1/4 teaspoon onion powder
- 1/4 teaspoon cayenne pepper

Preparation:
1. Place the fish fillet in a bowl. Pour the milk over the fish fillet.
2. Squeeze lemon slice over the fish. Marinate for 15 minutes.
3. Spread the mustard on the fish fillets.
4. In another bowl, mix the rest of the ingredients.
5. Coat the fish fillets with the cornmeal mixture. Place on the Ninja Foodi basket.
6. Set it to air crisp. Seal the crisping lid. Cook at 390 degrees for 10 minutes.
7. Flip the fillets and cook for 5 more minutes.

Serving Suggestion: Serve with fresh green salad.

Tip: You can use Dijon mustard or yellow mustard for this recipe.

Nutritional Information Per Serving:
Calories 595
Total Fat 24g
Saturated Fat 3.4g
Cholesterol 178mg
Sodium 184mg
Total Carbohydrate 28.4g
Dietary Fiber 4.5g
Total Sugars 4.8g

Protein 64.7g
Potassium 1221mg

6. Fish Sticks

Serves: 2
Preparation time: 20 minutes

Ingredients:

- 1 lb. cod, sliced into strips
- 1/2 cup tapioca starch
- 2 eggs
- 1 teaspoon dried dill
- Salt and pepper to taste
- 1 cup almond flour
- 1 teaspoon onion powder
- 1/2 teaspoon mustard powder
- 2 tablespoons avocado oil

Preparation:

1. Pat the cod fillet strips dry using paper towel.
2. Place the tapioca starch in a bowl.
3. In another bowl, beat the eggs.
4. In a larger bowl, mix the dill, salt, pepper, almond flour, onion powder and mustard powder. Dip each strip in the first, second and third bowls.
5. Coat the Ninja Foodi basket with the avocado oil.
6. Place the fish strips inside. Cook at 390 degrees F for 5 minutes.

Serving Suggestion: Serve with tartar sauce.

Tip: You can also freeze the fish sticks and cook frozen. Just increase cooking time to 7 to 10 minutes.

Nutritional Information Per Serving:

Calories 549
Total Fat 15g
Saturated Fat 2.6g
Cholesterol 288mg
Sodium 246mg
Total Carbohydrate 39.4g
Dietary Fiber 2.7g
Total Sugars 2.2g
Protein 61g

Potassium 695mg

7. Fish Fillet with Pesto Sauce

Serves: 3
Preparation time: 20 minutes

Ingredients:

- 3 white fish fillets
- 1 tablespoon olive oil
- Salt and pepper to taste
- 2 cups fresh basil leaves
- 2 cloves garlic, crushed
- 2 tablespoons pine nuts
- 1 tablespoon Parmesan cheese, grated
- 1 cup olive oil

Preparation:

1. Coat the fish fillets with 1 tablespoon of olive oil. Season with the salt and pepper.
2. Place in the Ninja Foodi basket. Cook at 320 degrees for 8 minutes.
3. While waiting, mix the remaining ingredients in a food processor.
4. Pulse until smooth. Spread the pesto sauce on both sides of the fish before serving.

Serving Suggestion: Garnish with chopped pine nuts.

Tip: Pesto sauce can be prepared in advanced and chilled in the refrigerator for up to 3 days.

Nutritional Information Per Serving:

Calories 383
Total Fat 22.6g
Saturated Fat 4.1g
Cholesterol 125mg
Sodium 188mg
Total Carbohydrate 2.2g
Dietary Fiber 0.5g
Total Sugars 0.3g
Protein 42.1g
Potassium 715mg

8. Coconut Shrimp

Serves: 4
Preparation time: 20 minutes

Ingredients:
- 1/2 cup all purpose flour
- 1-1/2 teaspoons black pepper
- 2 eggs
- 1/3 cup panko bread crumbs
- 2/3 cup unsweetened coconut flakes
- 12 oz. shrimp, peeled and deveined
- Cooking spray
- Salt and pepper to taste
- 1/4 cup honey
- 1/4 cup lime juice

Preparation:
1. Mix the flour and black pepper in a bowl. In another bowl, beat the egg.
2. In the third bowl, mix the bread crumbs and coconut flakes.
3. Dip each of the shrimp in the first, second and third bowls.
4. Place in the Ninja Foodi basket. Set it to air crisp. Cover the crisping lid.
5. Cook at 400 degrees F for 8 minutes, turn halfway through.
6. Season with the salt and pepper.
7. Mix the remaining ingredients and serve with the shrimp.

Serving Suggestion: Garnish with fresh cilantro.

Tip: Keep the tails of the shrimp.

Nutritional Information Per Serving:
Calories 293
Total Fat 4.4g
Saturated Fat 1.3g
Cholesterol 261mg
Sodium 306mg
Total Carbohydrate 37.8g
Dietary Fiber 1.1g
Total Sugars 18.2g
Protein 25.1g
Potassium 229mg

9. Hot Prawns

Serves: 4
Preparation time: 15 minutes

Ingredients:

- 1 teaspoon chili flakes
- 1 teaspoon chili powder
- Salt and pepper to taste
- 12 king prawns
- 3 tablespoons mayonnaise
- 1 tablespoon ketchup
- 1 tablespoon wine vinegar

Preparation:

1. Combine all the spices in a bowl. Toss the prawns in the spice mixture.
2. Place the prawns in the Ninja Foodi basket. Seal the crisping lid.
3. Choose air crisp function. Cook at 360 degrees for 8 minutes.
4. While waiting, mix the mayo, ketchup and vinegar. Serve with the prawns.

Serving Suggestion: Place prawns in cocktails glasses.

Nutritional Information Per Serving:

Calories 490
Total Fat 27.8g
Saturated Fat 11.4g
Cholesterol 3mg
Sodium 177mg
Total Carbohydrate 8.7g
Dietary Fiber 0.5g
Total Sugars 8.9g
Protein 0.3g
Potassium 29mg

10. Crispy Shrimp

Serves: 4
Preparation time: 20 minutes

Ingredients:

- 1 lb. shrimp, peeled and deveined
- 2 eggs

- 1/2 cup bread crumbs
- 1/2 cup onion, diced
- 1 teaspoon ginger
- 1 teaspoon garlic powder
- Salt and pepper to taste

Preparation:

1. In one bowl, beat the two eggs. In another bowl, put the rest of the ingredients.
2. Dip the shrimp first in the eggs and then in the spice mixture.
3. Place in the Ninja Foodi basket. Seal the crisping lid. Choose air crisp function.
4. Cook at 350 degrees for 10 minutes.

Serving Suggestion: Serve with chili sauce.

Tip: Keep the tails of the shrimp intact.

Nutritional Information Per Serving:

Calories 229
Total Fat 4.9g
Saturated Fat 1.4g
Cholesterol 321mg
Sodium 407mg
Total Carbohydrate 13.8g
Dietary Fiber 1.1g
Total Sugars 1.8g
Protein 30.7g
Potassium 283mg

11. Salt and Pepper Shrimp

Serves: 4
Preparation time: 20 minutes

Ingredients:

- 2 teaspoons peppercorns
- 1 teaspoon salt
- 1 teaspoons sugar
- 1 lb. shrimp
- 3 tablespoons rice flour
- 2 tablespoons oil

Preparation:

1. Set the Ninja Foodi to sauté. Roast the peppercorns for 1 minute. Let them cool.
2. Crush the peppercorns and add the salt and sugar.
3. Coat the shrimp with this mixture and then with flour.
4. Sprinkle oil on the Ninja Foodi basket. Place the shrimp on top.
5. Cook at 350 degrees for 10 minutes, flipping halfway through.

Serving Suggestion: Serve with fresh salad.

Tip: Add more peppercorns if you like it spicier.

Nutritional Information Per Serving:

Calories 228
Total Fat 8.9g
Saturated Fat 1.5g
Cholesterol 239mg
Sodium 859mg
Total Carbohydrate 9.3g
Dietary Fiber 0.5g
Total Sugars 1g
Protein 26.4g
Potassium 211mg

12. Tuna Patties

Serves: 2
Preparation time: 30 minutes

Ingredients:

- 2 cans tuna flakes
- 1/2 tablespoon almond flour
- 1 teaspoon dried dill
- 1 tablespoon mayo
- 1/2 teaspoon onion powder
- 1 teaspoon garlic powder
- Salt and pepper to taste
- 1 tablespoon lemon juice

Preparation:

1. Mix all the ingredients in a bowl. Form patties. Set the tuna patties on the Ninja Foodi basket. Seal the crisping lid. Set it to air crisp.

2. Cook at 400 degrees for 10 minutes. Flip and cook for 5 more minutes.

Serving Suggestion: Serve with fresh green salad.

Tip: Add more flour if too wet.

Nutritional Information Per Serving:

Calories 141
Total Fat 6.4g
Saturated Fat 0.7g
Cholesterol 17mg
Sodium 148mg
Total Carbohydrate 5.2g
Dietary Fiber 1g
Total Sugars 1.2g
Protein 17g
Potassium 48mg

13. Lemon Garlic Shrimp

Serves: 4
Preparation time: 40 minutes

Ingredients:

- 1 lb. shrimp, peeled and deveined
- 1 tablespoon olive oil
- 4 cloves garlic, minced
- 1 tablespoon lemon juice
- Salt to taste

Preparation:

1. Mix the olive oil, salt, lemon juice and garlic. Toss shrimp in the mixture.
2. Marinate for 15 minutes. Place the shrimp in the Ninja Foodi basket.
3. Seal the crisping lid. Select the air crisp setting.
4. Cook at 350 degrees for 8 minutes. Flip and cook for 2 more minutes.

Serving Suggestion: Sprinkle chopped parsley on top.

Tip: Add crushed red pepper flakes if you like it spicy.

Nutritional Information Per Serving:

Calories 170
Total Fat 5.5g
Saturated Fat 1.1g
Cholesterol 239mg

Sodium 317mg
Total Carbohydrate 2.8g
Dietary Fiber 0.1g
Total Sugars 0.1g
Protein 26.1g
Potassium 209mg

14. Crispy Cod Fish

Serves: 4
Preparation time: 30 minutes

Ingredients:

- 4 cod fish fillets
- Salt and sugar to taste
- 1 teaspoon sesame oil
- 250 ml water
- 5 tablespoons light soy sauce
- 1 teaspoon dark soy sauce
- 3 tablespoons oil
- 5 slices ginger

Preparation:

1. Pat the cod fish fillets dry.
2. Season with the salt, sugar and sesame oil. Marinate for 15 minutes.
3. Set the Ninja Foodi to air crisp.
4. Put the fish on top of the basket. Cook at 350 degrees F for 3 minutes.
5. Flip and cook for 2 minutes. Take the fish out and set aside.
6. Put the rest of the ingredients in the pot.
7. Set it to sauté. Simmer and pour over the fish before serving.

Serving Suggestion: Sprinkle top with chopped green onion.

Nutritional Information Per Serving:

Calories 303
Total Fat 13.1g
Saturated Fat 1.9g
Cholesterol 99mg
Sodium 144mg
Total Carbohydrate 2.9g
Dietary Fiber 0.5g
Total Sugars 0.1g

Protein 41.5g
Potassium 494mg

15. Crispy Fish Nuggets

Serves: 4
Preparation time: 30 minutes

Ingredients:

- 1 lb. cod fillet, sliced into 8 pieces
- Salt and pepper to taste
- 1/2 cup flour
- 1 tablespoon egg with 1 teaspoon water
- 1 cup bread crumbs
- 1 tablespoon vegetable oil

Preparation:

1. Season the fish with salt and pepper. Cover with the flour.
2. Dip the fish in the egg wash and into the bread crumbs.
3. Place the fish nuggets in the Ninja Foodi basket. Set it to air crisp function.
4. Seal with the crisping lid. Cook at 360 degrees for 15 minutes.

Serving Suggestion: Serve with lemon honey tartar sauce.

Tip: Add dried dill or garlic powder to the seasoning to make it tastier.

Nutritional Information Per Serving:

Calories 234
Total Fat 5.4g
Saturated Fat 1g
Cholesterol 25mg
Sodium 229mg
Total Carbohydrate 31.4g
Dietary Fiber 1.7g
Total Sugars 1.7g
Protein 14.1g
Potassium 70mg

16. Heartfelt Sesame Fish

(Prepping time: 8 minutes\ Cooking time: 8 minutes |For 4 servings)

Ingredients

- 1 and 1/2 pound salmon fillet

- 1 teaspoon sesame seeds
- 1 teaspoon butter, melted
- 1/2 teaspoon salt
- 1 tablespoon apple cider vinegar
- 1/4 teaspoon rosemary, dried

Directions

1. Take apple cider vinegar and spray it to the salmon fillets
2. Then add dried rosemary, sesame seeds, butter and salt
3. Mix them well. Take butter sauce and brush the salmon properly
4. Place the salmon on the rack and lower the air fryer lid. Set the air fryer mode
5. Cook the fish for 8 minutes at 360 F. Serve hot and enjoy!

Nutrition Values (Per Serving)

Calories: 239
Fat: 11.2g
Carbohydrates: 0.3g
Protein: 33.1g

17. Awesome Sock-Eye Salmon

(Prepping time: 5 minutes\ Cooking time: 5 minutes |For 4 servings)

Ingredients

- 4 sockeye salmon fillets
- 1 teaspoon Dijon mustard
- 1/4 teaspoon garlic, minced
- 1/4 teaspoon onion powder
- 1/4 teaspoon lemon pepper
- 1/2 teaspoon garlic powder
- 1/4 teaspoon salt
- 2 tablespoons olive oil
- 1 and 1/2 cup of water

Directions

1. Take a bowl and add mustard, lemon juice, onion powder, lemon pepper, garlic powder, salt, olive oil. Brush spice mix over salmon
2. Add water to Instant Pot. Place rack and place salmon fillets on rack
3. Lock lid and cook on LOW pressure for 7 minutes
4. Quick release pressure .Serve and enjoy!

Nutrition Values (Per Serving)

Calories: 353
Fat: 25g
Carbohydrates: 0.6g
Protein: 40g

18. Buttered Up Scallops

(Prepping time: 10 minutes\ Cooking time: 5 minutes |For 4 servings)

Ingredients

- 4 garlic cloves, minced
- 4 tablespoons rosemary, chopped
- 2 pounds sea scallops
- 12 cup butter
- Salt and pepper to taste

Directions

1. Set your Ninja Foodi to Saute mode and add butter, rosemary, and garlic
2. Saute for 1 minute. Add scallops, salt, and pepper
3. Saute for 2 minutes. Lock Crisping lid and Crisp for 3 minutes at 350 degrees F. Serve and enjoy!

Nutrition Values (Per Serving)

Calories: 279
Fat: 16g
Carbohydrates: 5g
Protein: 25g

19. Awesome Cherry Tomato Mackerel

(Prepping time: 5 minutes\ Cooking time: 7 minutes |For 4 servings)

Ingredients

- 4 Mackerel fillets
- 1/4 teaspoon onion powder
- 1/4 teaspoon lemon powder
- 1/4 teaspoon garlic powder
- 1/2 teaspoon salt
- 2 cups cherry tomatoes
- 3 tablespoons melted butter

- 1 and 1/2 cups of water
- 1 tablespoon black olives

Directions

1. Grease baking dish and arrange cherry tomatoes at the bottom of the dish
2. Top with fillets sprinkle all spices. Drizzle melted butter over
3. Add water to your Ninja Foodi
4. Lower rack in Ninja Foodi and place baking dish on top of the rack
5. Lock lid and cook on LOW pressure for 7 minutes . Quick release pressure. Serve and enjoy!

Nutrition Values (Per Serving)

Calories: 325
Fat: 24g
Carbohydrates: 2g
Protein: 21g

20. Lovely Air Fried Scallops

(Prepping time: 5 minutes\ Cooking time: 5 minutes |For 4 servings)

Ingredients

- 12 scallops
- 3 tablespoons olive oil
- Salt and pepper to taste

Directions

1. Gently rub scallops with salt, pepper, and oil
2. Transfer to your Ninja Foodie's insert, and place the insert in your Foodi
3. Lock Air Crisping lid and cook for 4 minutes at 390 degrees F
4. Half through, make sure to give them a nice flip and keep cooking. Serve warm and enjoy!

Nutrition Values (Per Serving)

Calories: 372
Fat: 11g
Carbohydrates: 0.9g
Protein: 63g

21. Packets Of Lemon And Dill Cod

(Prepping time: 10 minutes\ Cooking time: 5-10 minutes |For 4 servings)

Ingredients
- 2 tilapia cod fillets
- Salt, pepper and garlic powder to taste
- 2 sprigs fresh dill
- 4 slices lemon
- 2 tablespoons butter

Directions
1. Layout 2 large squares of parchment paper
2. Place fillet in center of each parchment square and season with salt, pepper and garlic powder
3. On each fillet, place 1 sprig of dill, 2 lemon slices, 1 tablespoon butter
4. Place trivet at the bottom of your Ninja Foodi. Add 1 cup water into the pot
5. Close parchment paper around fillets and fold to make a nice seal
6. Place both packets in your pot . Lock lid and cook on HIGH pressure for 5 minutes
7. Quick release pressure . Serve and enjoy!

Nutrition Values (Per Serving)
Calories: 259
Fat: 11g
Carbohydrates: 8g
Protein: 20g

22. Adventurous Sweet And Sour Fish

(Prepping time: 10 minutes\ Cooking time: 6 minutes |For 4 servings)

Ingredients
- 2 drops liquid stevia
- 1/4 cup butter
- 1 pound fish chunks
- 1 tablespoon vinegar
- Salt and pepper to taste

Directions
1. Set your Ninja Foodi to Saute mode and add butter, let it melt
2. Add fish chunks and Saute for 3 minutes. Add stevia, salt, and pepper, stir
3. Lock Crisping Lid and cook on "Air Crisp" mode for 3 minutes at 360 degrees F
4. Serve once done and enjoy!

Nutrition Values (Per Serving)
Calories: 274
Fat: 15g
Carbohydrates: 2g
Protein: 33g

23. Garlic And Lemon Prawn Delight

(Prepping time: 5 minutes\ Cooking time: 5 minutes |For 4 servings)

Ingredients
- 2 tablespoons olive oil
- 1 pound prawns
- 2 tablespoons garlic, minced
- 2/3 cup fish stock
- 1 tablespoon butter
- 2 tablespoons lemon juice
- 1 tablespoon lemon zest
- Salt and pepper to taste

Directions
1. Set your Ninja Foodi to Saute mode and add butter and oil, let it heat up
2. Stir in remaining ingredients. Lock lid and cook on LOW pressure for 5 minutes
3. Quick release pressure. Serve and enjoy!

Nutrition Values (Per Serving)
Calories: 236
Fat: 12g
Carbohydrates: 2g
Protein: 27g

24. Lovely Carb Soup

(Prepping time: 5 minutes\ Cooking time: 6-7 hours |For 4 servings)

Ingredients
- 1 cup crab meat, cubed
- 1 tablespoon garlic, minced
- Salt as needed
- Red chili flakes as needed
- 3 cups vegetable broth

- 1 teaspoon salt

Directions

1. Coat the crab cubes in lime juice and let them sit for a while
2. Add the all ingredients (including marinated crab meat) to your Ninja Foodi and lock lid
3. Cook on SLOW COOK MODE (MEDIUM) for 3 hours
4. Let it sit for a while
5. Unlock lid and set to Saute mode, simmer the soup for 5 minutes more on LOW
6. Stir and check to season. Enjoy!

Nutrition Values (Per Serving)

Calories: 201
Fat: 11g
Carbohydrates: 12g
Protein: 13g

25. The Rich Guy Lobster And Butter

(Prepping time: 15 minutes\ Cooking time: 20 minutes |For 4 servings)

Ingredients

- 6 Lobster Tails
- 4 garlic cloves,
- 1/4 cup butter

Directions

1. Preheat the Ninja Foodi to 400 degrees F at first
2. Open the lobster tails gently by using kitchen scissors
3. Remove the lobster meat gently from the shells but keep it inside the shells
4. Take a plate and place it
5. Add some butter in a pan and allow it melt
6. Put some garlic cloves in it and heat it over medium-low heat
7. Pour the garlic butter mixture all over the lobster tail meat
8. Let the fryer to broil the lobster at 130 degrees F
9. Remove the lobster meat from Ninja Foodi and set aside
10. Use a fork to pull out the lobster meat from the shells entirely
11. Pour some garlic butter over it if needed. Serve and enjoy!

Nutrition Values (Per Serving)
Calories: 160
Fat: 1g
Carbohydrates: 1g
Protein: 20g

26. Lovely Panko Cod

(Prepping time: 5 minutes\ Cooking time: 15 minutes |For 6 servings)

Ingredients
- 2 uncooked cod fillets, 6 ounces each
- 3 teaspoons kosher salt
- 3/4 cup panko bread crumbs
- 2 tablespoons butter, melted
- 1/4 cup fresh parsley, minced
- 1 lemon. Zested and juiced

Directions
1. Pre-heat your Ninja Foodi at 390 degrees F and place Air Crisper basket inside
2. Season cod and salt
3. Take a bowl and add bread crumbs, parsley, lemon juice, zest, butter, and mix well
4. Coat fillets with the bread crumbs mixture and place fillets in your Air Crisping basket
5. Lock Air Crisping lid and cook on Air Crisp mode for 15 minutes at 360 degrees F
6. Serve and enjoy!

Nutrition Values (Per Serving)
Calories: 554
Fat: 24g
Carbohydrates: 5g
Protein: 37g

27. Salmon Paprika

(Prepping time: 5 minutes\ Cooking time: 7 minutes |For 4 servings)

Ingredients

- 2 wild caught salmon fillets, 1 to 1 and ½ inches thick
- 2 teaspoons avocado oil
- 2 teaspoons paprika
- Salt and pepper to taste
- Green herbs to garnish

Directions

1. Season salmon fillets with salt, pepper, paprika, and olive oil
2. Place Crisping basket in your Ninja Foodi, and pre-heat your Ninja Foodie at 390 degrees F
3. Place insert insider your Foodi and place the fillet in the insert, lock Air Crisping lid and cook for 7 minutes. Once done, serve the fish with herbs on top. Enjoy!

Nutrition Values (Per Serving)

Calories: 249
Fat: 11g
Carbohydrates: 1.8g
Protein: 35g

28. Heartfelt Air Fried Scampi

(Prepping time: 5 minutes\ Cooking time: 5 minutes |For 4 servings)

Ingredients

4 tablespoons butter
1 tablespoon lemon juice
1 tablespoon garlic, minced
2 teaspoons red pepper flakes
1 tablespoon chives, chopped
1 tablespoon basil leaves, minced
2 tablespoons chicken stock
1 pound defrosted shrimp

Directions

1. Set your Foodi to Saute mode and add butter, let the butter melt and add red pepper flakes and garlic, Saute for 2 minutes
2. Transfer garlic to crisping basket, add remaining ingredients (including shrimp) to the basket

3. Return basket back to the Ninja Foodi and lock the Air Crisping lid, cook for 5 minutes at 390 degrees F. Once done, serve with a garnish of fresh basil

Nutrition Values (Per Serving)
Calories: 372
Fat: 11g
Carbohydrates: 0.9g
Protein: 63g

29. Ranch Warm Fillets

(Prepping time: 5 minutes\ Cooking time: 13 minutes |For 4 servings)

Ingredients
- 1/4 cup panko
- 1/2 packet ranch dressing mix powder
- 1 and 1/4 tablespoons vegetable oil
- 1 egg beaten
- 2 tilapia fillets
- A garnish of herbs and chilies

Directions
1. Pre-heat your Ninja Foodi with the Crisping Basket inside at 350 degrees F
2. Take a bowl and mix in ranch dressing and panko
3. Beat eggs in a shallow bowl and keep it on the side
4. Dip fillets in the eggs, then in the panko mix
5. Place fillets in your Ninja Foodie's insert and transfer insert to Ninja Foodi
6. Lock Air Crisping Lid and Air Crisp for 13 minutes at 350 degrees F
7. Garnish with chilies and herbs. Enjoy!

Nutrition Values (Per Serving)
Calories: 301
Fat: 12g
Carbohydrates: 1.5g
Protein: 28g

30. Alaskan Cod Divine

(Prepping time: 10 minutes\ Cooking time: 5-10 minutes |For 4 servings)

Ingredients

- 1 large fillet, Alaskan Cod (Frozen)
- 1 cup cherry tomatoes
- Salt and pepper to taste
- Seasoning as you need
- 2 tablespoons butter
- Olive oil as needed

Directions

1. Take an ovenproof dish small enough to fit inside your pot
2. Add tomatoes to the dish, cut large fish fillet into 2-3 serving pieces and lay them on top of tomatoes. Season with salt, pepper, and your seasoning
3. Top each fillet with 1 tablespoon butter and drizzle olive oil
4. Add 1 cup of water to the pot. Place trivet to the Ninja Foodi and place dish on the trivet
5. Lock lid and cook on HIGH pressure for 9 minutes. Release pressure naturally over 10 minutes
6. Serve and enjoy!

Nutrition Values (Per Serving)

Calories: 449
Fat: 32g
Carbohydrates: 11g
Protein: 25g

31. Kale And Salmon Delight

(Prepping time: 10 minutes\ Cooking time: 5 minutes |For 4 servings)

Ingredients

- 1 lemon, juiced
- 2 salmon fillets
- 1/4 cup extra virgin olive oil
- 1 teaspoon Dijon mustard
- 4 cups kale, thinly sliced, ribs removed
- 1 teaspoon salt
- 1 avocado, diced
- 1 cup pomegranate seeds
- 1 cup walnuts, toasted
- 1 cup goat parmesan cheese, shredded

Directions

1. Season salmon with salt and keep it on the side. Place a trivet in your Ninja Foodi
2. Place salmon over the trivet. Lock lid and cook on HIGH pressure for 15 minutes
3. Release pressure naturally over 10 minutes. Transfer salmon to a serving platter
4. Take a bowl and add kale, season with salt
5. Take another bowl and make the dressing by adding lemon juice, Dijon mustard, olive oil, and red wine vinegar. Season kale with dressing and add diced avocado, pomegranate seeds, walnuts and cheese. Toss and serve with the fish. Enjoy!

Nutrition Values (Per Serving)

Calories: 234
Fat: 14g
Carbohydrates: 12g
Protein: 16g

32. Breathtaking Cod Fillets

(Prepping time: 10 minutes\ Cooking time: 5-10 minutes |For 4 servings)

Ingredients

- 1 pound frozen cod fish fillets
- 2 garlic cloves, halved
- 1 cup chicken broth
- 1/2 cup packed parsley
- 2 tablespoons oregano
- 2 tablespoons almonds, sliced½ teaspoon paprika

Directions

1. Take the fish out of the freezer and let it defrost
2. Take a food processor and stir in garlic, oregano, parsley, paprika, 1 tablespoon almond and process. Set your Ninja Foodi to "SAUTE" mode and add olive oil, let it heat up
3. Add remaining almonds and toast, transfer to a towel. Pour broth in a pot and add herb mixture
4. Cut fish into 4 pieces and place in a steamer basket, transfer steamer basket to the pot

5. Lock lid and cook on HIGH pressure for 3 minutes. Quick release pressure once has done
6. Serve steamed fish by pouring over the sauce.Enjoy!

Nutrition Values (Per Serving)

Calories: 246
Fat: 10g
Carbohydrates: 8g
Protein: 15g

33. Lemon And Pepper Salmon Delight

(Prepping time: 5 minutes\ Cooking time: 6 minutes |For 4 servings)

Ingredients

- 3/4 cup of water
- Sprigs of parsley, basil, tarragon
- 1 pound salmon, skin on
- 3 teaspoons ghee
- 3/4 teaspoon salt
- 1/2 teaspoon pepper
- 1/2 lemon, sliced
- 1 red bell pepper, julienned
- 1 carrot, julienned

Directions

1. Set your Ninja Foodi to Saute mode and add water and herbs
2. Place a steamer rack and add the salmon. Drizzle ghee on top of the salmon
3. Season with pepper and salt. Cover lemon slices on top
4. Lock up the lid and cook on HIGH pressure for 3 minutes
5. Release the pressure naturally over 10 minutes
6. Transfer the salmon to a platter. Add veggies to your pot and set the pot to Saute mode
7. Cook for 1-2 minutes. Serve the cooked vegetables with salmon. Enjoy!

Nutrition Values (Per Serving)

Calories: 464
Fat: 34g
Carbohydrates: 3g
Protein: 34g

34. Fresh Steamed Salmon

(Prepping time: 5 minutes\ Cooking time: 5 minutes |For 4 servings)

Ingredients

- 2 salmon fillets
- 1/4 cup onion, chopped
- 2 stalks green onion stalks, chopped
- 1 whole egg
- Almond meal
- Salt and pepper to taste
- 2 tablespoons olive oil

Directions

1. Add a cup of water to your Ninja Foodi and place a steamer rack on top
2. Place the fish. Season the fish with salt and pepper and lock up the lid
3. Cook on HIGH pressure for 3 minutes. Once done, quick release the pressure
4. Remove the fish and allow it to cool
5. Break the fillets into a bowl and add egg, yellow and green onions
6. Add 1/2 a cup of almond meal and mix with your hand. Divide the mixture into patties
7. Take a large skillet and place it over medium heat. Add oil and cook the patties.Enjoy!

Nutrition Values (Per Serving)

Calories: 238
Fat: 15g
Carbohydrates: 1g
Protein: 23g

Vegan and Vegetarian Recipes

1. Fried Soy Curls

Serves: 2
Preparation time: 30 minutes

Ingredients:

- 4 oz. soy curls
- 3 cups hot water
- 1/4 cup fine ground cornmeal
- 1/4 cup nutritional yeast
- 1 teaspoon poultry seasoning
- 1 teaspoons Cajun seasoning
- Salt and pepper to taste

Preparation:

1. Soak the soy curls in hot water for 10 minutes. Drain in a strainer.
2. Press the water out. In a bowl, mix the rest of the ingredients.
3. Coat each soy curl with the breading. Place in the Ninja Foodi basket.
4. Seal the crisping lid. Set it to air crisp function.
5. Cook at 380 degrees for 5 minutes. Season with the salt and pepper.

Serving Suggestion: Serve with mashed potatoes and gravy.

Nutritional Information Per Serving:

Calories 100
Total Fat 1g
Saturated Fat 19g
Fiber 3g
Carbohydrates 17g
Protein 4g
Cholesterol 22mg
Sugars 2g
Sodium 19mg
Potassium 174mg

2. Crispy Tofu

Serves: 4
Preparation time: 1 hour

Ingredients:

- 1 teaspoon seasoned rice vinegar
- 2 tablespoons low sodium soy sauce
- 2 teaspoons toasted sesame oil
- 1 block firm tofu, sliced into cubes
- 1 tablespoon potato starch
- Cooking spray

Preparation:

1. In a bowl, mix the vinegar, soy sauce, and sesame oil.
2. Marinate the tofu for 30 minutes. Coat the tofu with potato starch.
3. Spray the Ninja Foodi basket with oil. Seal the crisping lid. Choose the air crisp setting. Cook at 370 degrees for 20 minutes, flipping halfway through.

Serving Suggestion: Serve with soy sauce and vinegar dipping sauce.

Tip: Press the tofu dry using paper towel.

Nutritional Information Per Serving:

Calories 137
Total Fat 3.4g
Saturated Fat 0.5g
Cholesterol 0mg
Sodium 310mg
Total Carbohydrate 24g
Dietary Fiber 0.5g
Total Sugars 0.4g
Protein 2.3g
Potassium 50mg

3. Onion Rings

Serves: 4
Preparation time: 30 minutes

Ingredients:

- 3 yellow onions, sliced into rings
- 1/2 cup almond flour

- 2/3 cup unsweetened coconut milk
- 1/2 teaspoon paprika
- 1/4 teaspoon turmeric
- Salt to taste

Preparation:

1. Mix all the ingredients except the onion rings in a large bowl.
2. Coat each onion ring with the mixture. Place in the Ninja Foodi basket.
3. Seal the crisping lid. Set it to air crisp.
4. Cook at 400 degrees for 10 minutes, flipping halfway through.

Serving Suggestion: Serve with ketchup or hot sauce.

Tip: This is best served warm.

Nutritional Information Per Serving:

Calories 147
Total Fat 11.3g
Saturated Fat 8.6g
Cholesterol 0mg
Sodium 49mg
Total Carbohydrate 10.9g
Dietary Fiber 3.2g
Total Sugars 4.9g
Protein 2.6g
Potassium 235mg

4. Potato Wedges

Serves: 4
Preparation time: 30 minutes

Ingredients:

- 1 lb. potatoes, sliced into wedges
- 1 teaspoon olive oil
- Salt and pepper to taste
- 1/2 teaspoon garlic powder

Preparation:

1. Coat the potatoes with oil. Season with the salt, pepper and garlic powder.
2. Add the potatoes in the Ninja Foodi basket. Cover with the crisping lid.

3. Set it to air crisp. Cook at 400 degrees F for 16 minutes, flipping halfway through.

Serving Suggestion: Serve with vegan cheese sauce.

Tip: Soak the potatoes in water then pat dry with paper towel.

Nutritional Information Per Serving:

Calories 179
Total Fat 2.6g
Saturated Fat 0.4g
Cholesterol 0mg
Sodium 14mg
Total Carbohydrate 36.2g
Dietary Fiber 5.5g
Total Sugars 2.8g
Protein 3.9g
Potassium 931mg

5. Buffalo Cauliflower

Serves: 4
Preparation time: 40 minutes

Ingredients:

- 1 head cauliflower, sliced into florets.
- 1 cup almond flour
- 1 teaspoon vegan bouillon granules
- 1/4 teaspoon paprika
- 1/4 teaspoon chili powder
- 1/4 teaspoon cayenne pepper
- 1/4 teaspoon dried chipotle chili flakes
- 1 cup soy milk
- Cooking spray
- 2 tablespoons vegan butter
- 1/2 cup hot sauce
- 2 cloves garlic, minced

Preparation:

1. Mix the almond flour, vegan bouillon granules, paprika, chili powder, cayenne pepper, and dried chipotle chile flakes. Gradually add the milk. Mix well.
2. Toss the cauliflower in the mixture. Spray the Ninja Foodi basket with oil.

3. Put the cauliflower on the basket. Cook at 390 degrees F for 20 minutes.
4. Turn the cauliflower halfway through. Take the cauliflower out of the pot. Set aside.
5. Set the pot to sauté. Heat the butter, garlic and hot sauce. Simmer for 5 minutes.
6. Pour over the cauliflower florets.

Serving Suggestion: Garnish with freshly parsley.

Tip: You can also use almond or hemp milk.

Nutritional Information Per Serving:

Calories 199
Total Fat 9.6g
Saturated Fat 0.9g
Cholesterol 0mg
Sodium 1634mg
Total Carbohydrate 20.2g
Dietary Fiber 6.1g
Total Sugars 8.9g
Protein 10.2g
Potassium 658mg

6. Garlic Chips

Serves: 2
Preparation time: 1 hour

Ingredients:

- 2 potatoes, sliced into chips
- Salt to taste
- 4 cloves garlic, minced
- 2 tablespoons vegan parmesan

Preparation:

1. Put the potatoes in a bowl of water. Stir in the salt. Soak for 20 to 30 minutes.
2. Drain the potatoes and pat try. Season with the garlic and vegan parmesan.
3. Arrange the chips on the Ninja Foodi basket. Seal the crisping lid.
4. Set it to air crisp function. Cook at 350 degrees for 10 minutes or until crispy.
5. Flip every 3 to 5 minutes.

Serving Suggestion: Serve with hot sauce or mayo.

Tip: Do not overcrowd to cook evenly.

Nutritional Information Per Serving:

Calories 156
Total Fat 0.2g
Saturated Fat 0.1g
Cholesterol 0mg
Sodium 91mg
Total Carbohydrate 35.4g
Dietary Fiber 5.2g
Total Sugars 2.5g
Protein 4g
Potassium 891mg

7. Cauliflower Stir Fry

Serves: 4
Preparation time: 30 minutes

Ingredients:

- 1 head cauliflower, sliced into florets
- 3/4 cup white onion, sliced
- 5 cloves garlic, minced
- 1-1/2 tablespoons tamari
- 1 tablespoon rice vinegar
- 1/2 teaspoon coconut sugar
- 1 tablespoon hot sauce

Preparation:

1. Put the cauliflower in the Ninja Foodi basket. Seal the crisping lid.
2. Select the air crisp setting. Cook at 350 degrees F for 10 minutes.
3. Add the onion, stir and cook for additional 10 minutes.
4. Add the garlic, and cook for 5 minutes. Mix the rest of the ingredients.
5. Pour over the cauliflower before serving.

Serving Suggestion: Garnish with chopped scallions.

Nutritional Information Per Serving:

Calories 93
Total Fat 3g
Sodium 510mg
Total Carbohydrates 12g

Dietary Fiber 3g
Sugars 4g
Protein 4g
Potassium 519mg

8. Vegan Cheese Sticks

Serves: 3-4
Preparation time: 8 hours and 30 minutes

Ingredients:

- 1 block vegan mozzarella, sliced into strips
- 1 bag vegan chips
- 1-1/2 cups almond flour
- 2 cups vegan milk
- 1/4 cup nutritional yeast

Preparation:

1. Put the chips and nutritional yeast in the food processor. Pulse until powdery.
2. Dip each cheese strip in the milk and cover with flour.
3. Dip into the milk again and coat with the powdered chips.
4. Place in the freezer for 8 hours. Add the frozen cheese sticks to the Ninja Foodi basket. Seal the crisping lid. Set it to air crisp. Cook at 380 degrees for 10 minutes.

Serving Suggestion: Serve with vegetable sticks.

Nutritional Information Per Serving:

Calories 116
Total Fat 4.1g
Saturated Fat 2.1g
Cholesterol 8mg
Sodium 87mg
Total Carbohydrate 9.7g
Dietary Fiber 5g
Total Sugars 0g
Protein 12.7g
Potassium 480mg

9. Smoked Chickpeas

Serves: 3
Preparation time: 30 minutes

Ingredients:

- 15 oz. chickpeas, rinsed and drained
- 1 tablespoon sunflower oil
- 2 tablespoons lemon juice
- 3/4 teaspoon smoked paprika
- 1/2 teaspoon granulated garlic
- 1/2 teaspoon ground cumin
- 1/4 teaspoon granulated onion
- Salt to taste

Preparation:

1. Mix all the ingredients except the oil and chickpeas. Put the chickpeas in the Ninja Foodi basket. Seal the crisping lid. Set it to air crisp function.
2. Cook at 390 degrees F for 15 minutes, shaking halfway through.
3. Put the chickpeas in the bowl of seasonings. Put them back to the Ninja Foodi basket.
4. Cook at 360 degrees F for 3 minutes.

Tip: You can also add cayenne pepper to make it spicier.

Nutritional Information Per Serving:

Calories 423
Total Fat 10.1g
Saturated Fat 1.1g
Cholesterol 0mg
Sodium 66mg
Total Carbohydrate 65.2g
Dietary Fiber 18.7g
Total Sugars 11.7g
Protein 20.8g
Potassium 957mg

10. Fried Broccoli

Serves: 2
Preparation time: 15 minutes

Ingredients:
- 4 cups broccoli florets
- 2 tablespoons coconut oil
- 1 tablespoon nutritional yeast
- Salt and pepper to taste

Preparation:
1. Combine all the ingredients in a bowl. Place the broccoli in the Ninja Foodi basket.
2. Seal the crisping lid. Choose air crisp setting. Cook at 370 degrees F for 5 minutes.

Serving Suggestion: Serve as side dish to main course.

Tip: Cook on a single layer to cook evenly.

Nutritional Information Per Serving:
Calories 197
Total Fat 14.5g
Saturated Fat 11.8g
Cholesterol 0mg
Sodium 63mg
Total Carbohydrate 14.4g
Dietary Fiber 6g
Total Sugars 3.1g
Protein 7.4g
Potassium 697mg

11. Tofu, Broccoli and Carrot

Serves: 2
Preparation time: 30 minutes

Ingredients:
- 1 block tofu, sliced into cubes
- 1 tablespoon sesame oil
- 1 tablespoon soy sauce
- 3 tablespoons tapioca starch
- 2 carrots, sliced into strips
- 1 cup broccoli florets
- 2 tablespoons orange zest
- 1/2 cup orange juice

- 3 tablespoons rice vinegar
- 1 tablespoon light soy sauce
- 1 tablespoon chicken stock
- 2 tablespoons sugar
- 2 teaspoons corn starch
- 2 cloves garlic, minced
- Salt to taste

Preparation:

1. Coat the tofu with the sesame oil and soy sauce. Cover with tapioca starch.
2. Put the tofu cubes in the Ninja Foodi basket. Seal the crisping lid.
3. Press air crisp. Cook at 390 degrees F for 5 minutes. Stir the tofu and cook for another 5 minutes. Take the tofu out of the pot. Mix the rest of the ingredients.
4. Set the pot to sauté. Add the broccoli and carrots with the mixture.
5. Put the tofu back. Simmer for 10 minutes.

Serving Suggestion: Serve with a bowl of hot rice.

Tip: You can also fry the broccoli and carrots if you like them crispy.

Nutritional Information Per Serving:

Calories 296
Total Fat 9g
Saturated Fat 1.4g
Cholesterol 0mg
Sodium 616mg
Total Carbohydrate 46.4g
Dietary Fiber 4.1g
Total Sugars 21.9g
Protein 6.8g
Potassium 575mg

12. Fried Tempeh

Serves: 4
Preparation time: 40 minutes

Ingredients:

- 200g tempeh, sliced into chunks
- 2 tablespoons vegan mayonnaise
- 3 tablespoons bread crumbs

Sauce:
- 2 tablespoons Korean red pepper paste
- 2 cloves garlic, crushed
- 1 tablespoon maple syrup
- 1 tablespoon soy sauce
- 1 tablespoon water
- Salt and pepper to taste

Preparation:
1. Put the mayo in one bowl and the bread crumbs in another. Dilute the mayo with water. Coat each tempeh with mayo and then with the bread crumbs.
2. Place in the Ninja Foodi basket. Seal the crisping lid. Set it to air crisp.
3. Cook at 350 degrees F for 15 minutes or until golden and crispy.
4. Stir every 5 minutes. Take them out and set aside.
5. Mix all the sauce ingredients. Put in the pot. Set it to sauté. Simmer for 5 minutes. Add the tempeh to the sauce and toss to coat evenly.

Serving Suggestion: Top with sesame seeds.

Tip: Cook in batches for even browning.

Nutritional Information Per Serving:
Calories 131
Total Fat 7.2g
Saturated Fat 1.1g
Cholesterol 0mg
Sodium 286mg
Total Carbohydrate 9.4g
Dietary Fiber 0.1g
Total Sugars 3.1g
Protein 9.6g
Potassium 231mg

13. Garlic Pepper Potato Chips

Serves: 2
Preparation time: 20 minutes

Ingredients:
- 1 large potato, sliced into thin chips
- Cooking spray

- Salt and garlic powder to taste
- 1 teaspoon black pepper

Preparation:

1. Spray oil on the Ninja Foodi basket.
2. Season the potato with the salt, garlic powder and black pepper.
3. Place potato chips on the basket. Seal the crisping lid. Set it to air crisp.
4. Cook at 450 degrees F for 10 minutes or until golden and crispy.

Serving Suggestion: Serve with mayo dip.

Tip: Press moisture out of the potatoes using paper towel.

Nutritional Information Per Serving:

Calories 147
Total Fat 0.5g
Saturated Fat 0.1g
Cholesterol 0mg
Sodium 12mg
Total Carbohydrate 32.9g
Dietary Fiber 4.3g
Total Sugars 1.5g
Protein 3.8g
Potassium 790mg

14. Brussels Sprouts

Serves: 4
Preparation time: 20 minutes

Ingredients:

- 1 lb. Brussels sprouts
- 2 teaspoons olive oil
- 1/4 teaspoon garlic powder
- 1/4 teaspoon salt

Preparation:

1. Put the Brussels sprouts in a bowl. Pour the olive oil into the bowl.
2. Season the sprouts with garlic powder and salt. Put the sprouts on the basket.
3. Seal the crisping lid. Set it to air crisp function.
4. Cook at 370 degrees F for 6 minutes, flipping halfway through.

Serving Suggestion: Serve as side dish to a main course.

Tip: Trim the brown leaves of the Brussels sprouts.

Nutritional Information Per Serving:

Calories 139
Total Fat 5.4g
Saturated Fat 0.9g
Cholesterol 0mg
Sodium 347mg
Total Carbohydrate 20.9g
Dietary Fiber 8.5g
Total Sugars 5g
Protein 7.8g
Potassium 885mg

15. Vegetable Fritters

Serves: 6
Preparation time: 30 minutes

Ingredients:

- 3 tablespoons ground flaxseed mixed with 1/2 cup water
- 2 potatoes, shredded
- 2 cups frozen mixed vegetables
- 1 cup frozen peas, thawed
- 1/2 cup onion, chopped
- 1/4 cup fresh cilantro, chopped
- 1/2 cup almond flour
- Salt to taste
- Cooking spray

Preparation:

1. Combine all the ingredients in a bowl. Form patties. Spray each patty with oil.
2. Transfer to the Ninja Foodi basket. Set it to air crisp. Close the crisping lid.
3. Cook at 360 degrees F for 15 minutes, flipping halfway through.

Tip: You can also omit the cooking spray for an oil-free recipe.

Nutritional Information Per Serving:

Calories 171
Total Fat 0.5g
Saturated Fat 0.1g

Cholesterol 0mg
Sodium 107mg
Total Carbohydrate 35.7g
Dietary Fiber 9.1g
Total Sugars 6.5g
Iron 2mg

16. Crazy Fresh Onion Soup

(Prepping time: 5 minutes\ Cooking time: 10-15 minutes |For 4 servings)

Ingredients

- 2 tablespoons avocado oil
- 8 cups yellow onion
- 1 tablespoon balsamic vinegar
- 6 cups of pork stock
- 1 teaspoon salt
- 2 bay leaves
- 2 large sprigs, fresh thyme

Directions

1. Cut up the onion in half through the root
2. Peel them and slice into thin half moons
3. Set the pot to Saute mode and add oil, one the oil is hot and add onions
4. Cook for about 15 minutes
5. Add balsamic vinegar and scrape any fond from the bottom
6. Add stock, bay leaves, salt, and thyme
7. Lock up the lid and cook on HIGH pressure for 10 minutes
8. Release the pressure naturally
9. Discard the bay leaf and thyme stems
10. Blend the soup using an immersion blender and serve!

Nutrition Values (Per Serving)

Calories: 454
Fat: 31g
Carbohydrates: 7g
Protein: 27g

17. Elegant Zero Crust Kale And Mushroom Quiche

(Prepping time: 5 minutes\ Cooking time: 9 hours |For 6 servings)

Ingredients

- 6 large eggs
- 2 tablespoons unsweetened almond milk
- 2 ounces low –fat feta cheese, crumbled
- 1/4 cup parmesan cheese, grated
- 1 and 1/2 teaspoons Italian seasoning
- 4 ounces mushrooms, sliced
- 2 cups kale, chopped

Directions

1. Grease the inner pot of your Ninja Foodi
2. Take a large bowl and whisk in eggs, cheese, almond milk, seasoning and mix it well
3. Stir in kale and mushrooms. Pour the mix into Ninja Foodi. Gently stir
4. Place lid and cook on SLOW COOK Mode(LOW) for 8-9 hours. Serve and enjoy!

Nutrition Values (Per Serving)

Calories: 112
Fat: 7g
Carbohydrates: 4g
Protein: 10g

18. Delicious Beet Borscht

(Prepping time: 5 minutes\ Cooking time: 45 minutes |For 6 servings)

Ingredients

- 8 cups beets
- 1/2 cup celery, diced
- 1/2 cup carrots, diced
- 2 garlic cloves, diced
- 1 medium onion, diced
- 3 cups cabbage, shredded
- 6 cups beef stock
- 1 bay leaf
- 1 tablespoon salt
- 1/2 tablespoon thyme
- 1/4 cup fresh dill, chopped
- 1/2 cup of coconut yogurt

Directions

1. Add the washed beets to a steamer in the Ninja Foodi
2. Add 1 cup of water. Steam for 7 minutes
3. Perform a quick release and drop into an ice bath
4. Carefully peel off the skin and dice the beets
5. Transfer the diced beets, celery, carrots, onion, garlic, cabbage, stock, bay leaf, thyme and salt to your Instant Pot. Lock up the lid and set the pot to SOUP mode, cook for 45 minutes
6. Release the pressure naturally. Transfer to bowls and top with a dollop of dairy-free yogurt
7. Enjoy with a garnish of fresh dill!

Nutrition Values (Per Serving)

Calories: 625
Fats: 46g
Carbs:19g
Protein:90g

19. Pepper Jack Cauliflower Meal

(Prepping time: 5 minutes\ Cooking time: 3 hours 35 minutes |For 6 servings)

Ingredients

- 1 head cauliflower
- 1/4 cup whipping cream
- 4 ounces cream cheese
- 1/2 teaspoon pepper
- 1 teaspoon salt
- 2 tablespoons butter
- 4 ounces pepper jack cheese
- 6 bacon slices, crumbled

Directions

1. Grease Ninja Foodi and add listed ingredients (except cheese and bacon)
2. Stir and Lock lid, cook SLOW COOK MODE (LOW) for 3 hours
3. Remove lid and add cheese, stir. Lock lid again and cook for 1 hour more
4. Garnish with bacon crumbles and enjoy!

Nutrition Values (Per Serving)

Calories: 272
Fat: 21g

Carbohydrates: 5g
Protein: 10g

20. Slow-Cooked Brussels

(Prepping time: 5 minutes\ Cooking time: 4 hours |For 4 servings)

Ingredients

- 1 pound Brussels sprouts, bottom trimmed and cut
- 1 tablespoon olive oil
- 1 -1/2 tablespoon Dijon mustard
- 1/4 cup of water
- Salt and pepper as needed
- 1/2 teaspoon dried tarragon

Directions

1. Add Brussels, salt, water, pepper, mustard to Ninja Foodi
2. Add dried tarragon and stir
3. Lock lid and cook on SLOW COOK MODE (LOW) for 5 hours until the Brussels are tender
4. Stir well and add Dijon over Brussels. Stir and enjoy!

Nutrition Values (Per Serving)

Calories: 83
Fat: 4g
Carbohydrates: 11g
Protein: 4g

21. Slowly Cooked Lemon Artichokes

(Prepping time: 10 minutes\ Cooking time: 5 hours |For 4 servings)

Ingredients

- 5 large artichokes
- 1 teaspoon of sea salt
- 2 stalks celery, sliced
- 2 large carrots, cut into matchsticks
- Juice from 1/2 a lemon
- 1/4 teaspoon black pepper
- 1 teaspoon dried thyme
- 1 tablespoon dried rosemary
- Lemon wedges for garnish

Directions

1. Remove the stalk from your artichokes and remove the tough outer shell
2. Transfer the chokes to your Ninja Foodi and add 2 cups of boiling water
3. Add celery, lemon juice, salt, carrots, black pepper, thyme, rosemary
4. Cook on Slow Cook mode (HIGH) for 4-5 hours
5. Serve the artichokes with lemon wedges. Serve and enjoy!

Nutrition Values (Per Serving)

Calories: 205
Fat: 2g
Carbohydrates: 12g
Protein: 34g

22. Well Dressed Brussels

(Prepping time: 10 minutes\ Cooking time: 4-5 hours |For 4 servings)

Ingredients

- 2 pounds Brussels, halved
- 2 red onions, sliced
- 2 tablespoons apple cider vinegar
- 1 tablespoon extra-virgin olive oil
- 1 teaspoon ground cinnamon
- 1/2 cup pecans, chopped

Directions

1. Add Brussels and onions to Ninja Foodi. Take a small bowl and add cinnamon, vinegar, olive oil
2. Pour mixture over sprouts and toss
3. Place lid and cook on SLOW COOK MODE (LOW) for 4-5 hours. Enjoy!

Nutrition Values (Per Serving)

Calories: 176
Fat: 10g
Carbohydrates: 14g
Protein: 4g

23. Cheddar Cauliflower Bowl

(Prepping time: 10 minutes\ Cooking time: 5 minutes |For 8 servings)

Ingredients

- 1/4 cup butter
- 1/2 sweet onion, chopped
- 1 head cauliflower, chopped
- 4 cups herbed vegetable stock
- 1/2 teaspoon ground nutmeg
- 1 cup heavy whip cream
- Salt and pepper as needed
- 1 cup cheddar cheese, shredded

Directions

1. Set your Ninja Foodi to sauté mode and add butter, let it heat up and melt
2. Add onion and Cauliflower, Saute for 10 minutes until tender and lightly browned
3. Add vegetable stock and nutmeg, bring to a boil
4. Lock lid and cook on HIGH pressure for 5 minutes, quick release pressure once done
5. Remove pot and from Foodi and stir in heavy cream, puree using an immersion blender
6. Season with more salt and pepper and serve with a topping of cheddar. Enjoy!

Nutrition Values (Per Serving)

Calories: 227
Fat: 21g
Carbohydrates: 4g
Protein: 8g

24. A Prosciutto And Thyme Eggs

(Prepping time: 10 minutes\ Cooking time: 5 minutes |For 4 servings)

Ingredients

- 4 kale leaves
- 4 prosciutto slices
- 3 tablespoons heavy cream
- 4 hardboiled eggs
- 1/4 teaspoon pepper
- 1/4 teaspoon salt
- 1 and 1/2 cups of water

Directions

1. Peel eggs and wrap in kale. Wrap in prosciutto and sprinkle salt and pepper
2. Add water to your Ninja Foodi and lower trivet. Place eggs inside and lock lid
3. Cook on HIGH pressure for 5 minutes. Quick release pressure. Serve and enjoy!

Nutrition Values (Per Serving)

Calories: 290
Fat: 23g
Carbohydrates: 4g
Protein: 16g

25. The Authentic Zucchini Pesto Meal

(Prepping time: 10 minutes\ Cooking time: 10 minutes |For 4 servings)

Ingredients

- 1 tablespoon olive oil
- 1 onion, chopped
- 2 and 1/2 pound roughly chopped zucchini
- 1/2 cup of water
- 1 and 1/2 teaspoon salt
- 1 bunch basil leaves
- 2 garlic cloves, minced
- 1 tablespoon extra-virgin olive oil
- Zucchini for making zoodles

Direction

1. Set the Ninja Foodi to Saute mode and add olive oil
2. Once the oil is hot, add onion and Saute for 4 minutes
3. Add zucchini, water, and salt. Lock up the lid and cook on HIGH pressure for 3 minutes
4. Release the pressure naturally. Add basil, garlic, and leaves
5. Use an immersion blender to blend everything well until you have a sauce-like consistency
6. Take the extra zucchini and pass them through a Spiralizer to get noodle like shapes
7. Toss the Zoodles with sauce and enjoy!

Nutrition Values (Per Serving)
Calories: 71
Fat: 4g
Carbohydrates: 6g
Protein: 3g

26. Supreme Cauliflower Soup

(Prepping time: 10 minutes\ Cooking time: 5 minutes |For 4 servings)

Ingredients
- 1/2 a small onion, chopped
- 2 tablespoons butter
- 1 large head of cauliflower, leaves and stems removed, coarsely chopped
- 2 cups chicken stock
- 1 teaspoon garlic powder
- 1 teaspoon salt
- 4 ounces cream cheese, cut into cubes
- 1 cup sharp cheddar cheese, cut
- 1/2 cup cream
- Extra cheddar, sour cream bacon strips, green onion for topping

Directions
1. Peel the onion and chop up into small pieces
2. Cut the leaves of the cauliflower and steam, making sure to keep the core intact
3. Coarsely chop the cauliflower into pieces
4. Set your Ninja Foodi to Saute mode and add onion, cook for 2-3 minutes
5. Add chopped cauliflower, stock, salt, and garlic powder
6. Lock up the lid and cook on HIGH pressure for 5 minutes. Perform a quick release
7. Prepare the toppings. Use an immersion blender to puree your soup in the Ninja Foodi
8. Serve your soup with a topping of sliced green onions, cheddar, crumbled bacon. Enjoy!

Nutrition Values (Per Serving)
Calories: 438
Fat: 36g
Carbohydrates: 8g
Protein: 22g

27. Very Rich And Creamy Asparagus Soup

(Prepping time: 10 minutes\ Cooking time: 5-10 minutes |For 4 servings)

Ingredients

- 1 tablespoon olive oil
- 3 green onions, sliced crosswise into ¼ inch pieces
- 1 pound asparagus, tough ends removed, cut into 1 inch pieces
- 4 cups vegetable stock
- 1 tablespoon unsalted butter
- 1 tablespoon almond flour
- 2 teaspoon salt
- 1 teaspoon white pepper
- 1/2 cup heavy cream

Directions

1. Set your Ninja Foodi to "Saute" mode and add oil, let it heat up
2. Add green onions and Saute for a few minutes, add asparagus and stock
3. Lock lid and cook on HIGH pressure for 5 minutes
4. Take a small saucepan and place it over low heat, add butter, flour and stir until the mixture foams and turns into a golden beige, this is your blond roux
5. Remove from heat. Release pressure naturally over 10 minutes
6. Open the lid and add roux, salt, and pepper to the soup
7. Use an immersion blender to puree the soup
8. Taste and season accordingly, swirl in cream and enjoy!

Nutrition Values (Per Serving)

Calories: 192
Fat: 14g
Carbohydrates: 8g
Protein: 6g

28. Summertime Vegetable Platter

(Prepping time: 5 minutes\ Cooking time: 3 hours 5 minutes |For 6 servings)

Ingredients

- 1 cup grape tomatoes
- 2 cups okra
- 1 cup mushrooms

- 2 cups yellow bell peppers
- 1 and 1/2 cup red onions
- 2 and 1/2 cups zucchini
- 1/2 cup olive oil
- 1/2 cup balsamic vinegar
- 1 tablespoon fresh thyme, chopped
- 2 tablespoons fresh basil, chopped

Directions

1. Slice and chop okra, onions, tomatoes, zucchini, mushrooms
2. Add veggies to a large container and mix
3. Take another dish and add oil and vinegar, mix in thyme and basil
4. Toss the veggies into Ninja Foodi and pour marinade. Stir well
5. Close lid and cook on 3 hours on SLOW COOK MOD (HIGH), making sure to stir after every hour

Nutrition Values (Per Serving)

Calories: 233
Fat: 18g
Carbohydrates: 14g
Protein: 3g

29. The Creative Mushroom Stroganoff

(Prepping time: 5 minutes\ Cooking time: 10 minutes |For 6 servings)

Ingredients

- 1/4 cup unsalted butter, cubed
- 1 pound cremini mushrooms, halved
- 1 large onion, halved
- 4 garlic cloves, minced
- 2 cups vegetable broth
- 1/2 teaspoon salt
- 1/4 teaspoon fresh black pepper
- 1 and 1/2 cups sour cream
- 1/4 cup fresh flat-leaf parsley, chopped
- 1 cup grated parmesan cheese

Directions

1. Add butter, mushrooms, onion, garlic, vegetable broth, salt, pepper, and paprika

2. Gently stir and lock lid. Cook on HIGH pressure for 5 minutes
3. Release pressure naturally over 10 minutes
4. Serve by stirring in sour cream and with a garnish of parsley and parmesan cheese. Enjoy!

Nutrition Values (Per Serving)

Calories: 453
Fat: 37g
Carbohydrates: 11g
Protein: 19g

30. Garlic And Ginger Red Cabbage Platter

(Prepping time: 10 minutes\ Cooking time: 8 minutes |For 6 servings)

Ingredients

- 2 tablespoon coconut oil
- 1 tablespoon butter
- 3 garlic cloves, crushed
- 2 teaspoon fresh ginger, grated
- 8 cups red cabbage, shredded
- 1 teaspoon salt
- 1/2 a teaspoon pepper
- 1/3 cup water

Directions

1. Set your Ninja Foodi to Saute mode and add coconut oil and butter, allow to heat up
2. Add garlic and ginger and mix. Add cabbage, pepper, salt, and water
3. Mix well and lock up the lid, cook on HIGH pressure for 5 minutes
4. Perform a quick release and mix. Serve and enjoy!

Nutrition Values (Per Serving)

Calories: 96
Fat: 6g
Carbohydrates: 9g
Protein: 1.8g

31. The Veggie Lover's Onion And Tofu Platter

(Prepping time: 8 minutes\ Cooking time: 12 minutes |For 4 servings)

Ingredients

- 4 tablespoons butter
- 2 tofu blocks, pressed and cubed into 1-inch pieces
- Salt and pepper to taste
- 1 cup cheddar cheese, grated
- 2 medium onions, sliced

Directions

1. Take a bowl and add tofu, season with salt and pepper
2. Set your Foodi to Saute mode and add butter, let it melt
3. Add onions and Saute for 3 minutes. Add seasoned tofu and cook for 2 minutes more
4. Add cheddar and gently stir
5. Lock the lid and bring down the Air Crisp mode, let the dish cook on "Air Crisp" mode for 3 minutes at 340 degrees F. Once done, take the dish out, serve and enjoy!

Nutrition Values (Per Serving)

Calories: 184
Fat: 12g
Carbohydrates: 5g
Protein: 12g

32. Feisty Maple Dredged Carrots

(Prepping time: 10 minutes\ Cooking time: 4 minutes |For 6 servings)

Ingredients

- 2-pound carrot
- 1/4 cup raisins
- Pepper as needed
- 1 cup of water
- 1 tablespoon butter
- 1 tablespoon sugar-free Keto friendly maple syrup

Directions

1. Wash, peel the skin and slice the carrots diagonally
2. Add the carrots, raisins, water to your Ninja Foodi
3. Lock up the lid and cook on HIGH pressure for 4 minutes. Perform a quick release

4. Strain the carrots . Add butter and maple syrup to the warm Ninja Foodi and mix well
   5. Transfer the strained carrots back to the pot and stir to coat with maple sauce and butter
   6. Serve with a bit of pepper. Enjoy!

Nutrition Values (Per Serving)

Calories: 358
Fats: 12g
Carbs: 20g
Protein: 1g

33. The Original Sicilian Cauliflower Roast

(Prepping time: 10 minutes\ Cooking time: 10 minutes |For 4 servings)

Ingredients

- 1 medium cauliflower head, leaves removed
- 1/4 cup olive oil
- 1 teaspoon red pepper, crushed
- 1/2 cup of water
- 2 tablespoons capers, rinsed and minced
- 1/2 cup parmesan cheese, grated
- 1 tablespoon fresh parsley, chopped

Directions

1. Take the Ninja Foodi and start by adding water and place the cook and crisp basket inside the pot. Cut an "X" on the head of cauliflower by using a knife and slice it about halfway down
2. Take a basket and transfer the cauliflower in it
3. Then put on the pressure lid and seal it and set it on low pressure for 3 minutes
4. Add olive oil, capers, garlic, and crushed red pepper into it and mix them well
5. Once the cauliflower is cooked, do a quick release and remove the lid
6. Pour in the oil and spice mixture on the cauliflower
7. Spread equally on the surface then sprinkle some Parmesan cheese from the top
8. Close the pot with crisping lid. Set it on Air Crisp mode to 390 degrees F for 10 minutes

9. Once done, remove the cauliflower flower the Ninja Foodi transfer it into a serving plate
10. Cut it up into pieces and transfer them to serving plates. Sprinkle fresh parsley from the top
11. Serve and enjoy!

Nutrition Values (Per Serving)

Calories: 119
Fat: 10g
Carbohydrates: 5g
Protein: 2.2g

Grains and Beans

1. Fried Green Beans

Serves: 1
Preparation time: 15 minutes

Ingredients:

- 1 cup green beans
- 1 tablespoon avocado oil
- 2 tablespoons bread crumbs
- Salt and pepper to taste

Preparation:

1. Toss the green beans in oil. Season with the salt and pepper.
2. Coat with the bread crumbs. Cook at 390 degrees F for 8 minutes.
3. Flip and cook for 2 more minutes.

Serving Suggestion: Serve as side dish to main course.

Nutritional Information Per Serving:

Calories 106
Total Fat 2.6g
Saturated Fat 0.6g
Cholesterol 0mg
Sodium 106mg
Total Carbohydrate 18.4g
Dietary Fiber 5g
Total Sugars 2.4g
Protein 4g
Potassium 302mg

2. Navy Beans with Ham

Serves: 10
Preparation time: 40 minutes

Ingredients:

- 1 tablespoon olive oil
- 1 onion, chopped

- 2 carrot, shredded
- 2 tablespoons garlic, minced
- 2 stalks celery, chopped
- 6 cups chicken stock
- 24 oz. dried navy beans
- 1 teaspoon ground thyme
- 1 teaspoon paprika
- 1 lb. cooked ham, sliced into small cubes
- 14 oz. canned diced tomatoes
- Salt and pepper to taste

Preparation:

1. Set the Ninja Foodi to sauté. Pour in the oil. Cook the onion and carrot for 2 minutes.
2. Add the garlic and celery. Cook for 3 minutes.
3. Stir in the rest of the ingredients except the ham and tomatoes. Cover the pot.
4. Set it to pressure. Cook at high pressure for 10 minutes.
5. Release the pressure naturally. Stir in the tomatoes and ham.
6. Simmer for 5 minutes by pressing sauté function.

Serving Suggestion: Serve with crusty bread.

Nutritional Information Per Serving:

Calories 342
Total Fat 6.8g
Saturated Fat 1.7g
Cholesterol 26mg
Sodium 1067mg
Total Carbohydrate 48.1g
Dietary Fiber 18.4g
Total Sugars 5.3g
Protein 23.9g
Potassium 1116mg

3. Roasted Chickpeas

Serves: 2
Preparation time: 30 minutes

Ingredients:

- 1 can chickpeas, rinsed and drained
- 2 teaspoons olive oil

- 1 teaspoon garlic powder
- 1 teaspoon ground cumin
- 1 teaspoon ground coriander
- 1/8 tsp. ground ginger

Preparation:
1. Coat the beans with oil. Season with all the spices. Place in the Ninja Foodi basket.
2. Seal the crisping lid. Set it to air crisp. Cook at 370 degrees F for 12 minutes.
3. Stir the chickpeas and cook for another 8 minutes.
4. Stir once more and cook for 1 more minute.

Serving Suggestion: Mix with other nuts and seeds.

Tip: Roasted chickpeas can be stored in an airtight jar or resealable plastic bag.

Nutritional Information Per Serving:
Calories 207
Total Fat 5.5g
Saturated Fat 0.7g
Cholesterol 0mg
Sodium 13mg
Total Carbohydrate 31.1g
Dietary Fiber 8.8g
Total Sugars 5.5g
Protein 9.9g
Potassium 456mg

4. Spicy Green Beans

Serves: 4
Preparation time: 30 minutes

Ingredients:
- 12 oz. fresh green beans, trimmed
- 1 tablespoon sesame oil
- 1 teaspoon soy sauce
- 1 teaspoon rice wine vinegar
- 1 clove garlic, minced
- 1/2 teaspoon red pepper flakes

Preparation:
1. Mix all the ingredients in a large bowl. Marinate for 5 minutes.
2. Place the green beans in the Ninja Foodi basket. Seal the crisping lid.

3. Set it to air crisp. Cook at 400 degrees F for 12 minutes, flipping halfway through.

Serving Suggestion: Sprinkle toasted garlic chips on top.

Tip: Use low sodium soy sauce

Nutritional Information Per Serving:

Calories 59
Total Fat 3.6g
Saturated Fat 1.0g
Cholesterol 0mg
Sodium 80mg
Total Carbohydrates 6.6g
Dietary Fiber 3g 12 %
Protein 1.7g
Sugars 1g
Potassium 192mg

5. Baked Beans

Serves: 12
Preparation time: 1 hour and 30 minutes

Ingredients:

- 16 oz. pinto beans
- 8 cups water
- Salt to taste
- 8 slices bacon
- 1 onion, chopped
- 1/2 red bell pepper, chopped
- 2/3 cup barbecue sauce
- 1/2 cup ketchup
- 2 tablespoons mustard
- 1/4 cup cider vinegar
- 1 teaspoon liquid smoke
- 1/2 cup light brown sugar
- 1/2 cup water

Preparation:

1. Add the beans, 8 cups of water and salt in the Ninja Foodi. Cover the pot.
2. Set it to pressure. Cook at high pressure for 25 minutes.
3. Release the pressure naturally. Drain the beans and rinse with cold water.
4. Set the Ninja Foodi to sauté. Add the bacon and cook until crispy.

5. Add the bell pepper and onion. Cook for 3 minutes.
6. Add the rest of the ingredients. Cover the pot. Set it to pressure. Cook at high pressure for 15 minutes. Release the pressure naturally.

Serving Suggestion: Top with croutons.

Nutritional Information Per Serving:

Calories 268
Total Fat 6.4g
Saturated Fat 1.9g
Cholesterol 14mg
Sodium 583mg
Total Carbohydrate 39.2g
Dietary Fiber 6.5g
Total Sugars 13.4g
Protein 13.6g
Potassium 714mg

6. Sausage & Beans

Serves: 8
Preparation time: 1 hour

Ingredients:

- 2 teaspoons olive oil
- 1-1/2 lb. smoked turkey sausage, sliced into rounds
- 1 onion, chopped
- 3 stalks celery, chopped
- 1 bay leaf
- 4 carrot, chopped
- 1 sprig fresh rosemary
- 4 sprigs fresh thyme
- 4 cloves garlic, minced
- 1/4 teaspoon oregano, dried
- 1/2 teaspoon pepper
- 6 cups chicken broth
- 1 lb. white beans

Preparation:

1. Set the Ninja Foodi to sauté. Pour in the olive oil. Add the sausage.
2. Brown both sides. Add the onion, celery, bay leaf and carrot.
3. Cook for 3 minutes. Add the rosemary, thyme, garlic and oregano.
4. Cook for 1 minute. Add the pepper and stir in broth. Simmer for 5 minutes.

5. Stir in the white beans. Lock the lid in place. Set it to pressure.
6. Cook at high pressure for 40 minutes. Release the pressure naturally.

Serving Suggestion: Serve with crusty bread.

Tip: You can soak the beans in water for 8 hours and reduce cooking time to 25 minutes.

Nutritional Information Per Serving:

Calories 268
Total Fat 3.8g
Saturated Fat 0.9g
Cholesterol 7mg
Sodium 708mg
Total Carbohydrate 40.7g
Dietary Fiber 10.1g
Total Sugars 4.2g
Protein 19.1g
Potassium 1342mg

7. Tomato & Beans

Serves: 6
Preparation time: 1 hour and 20 minutes

Ingredients:
- 4 slices bacon, chopped
- 1 onion, chopped
- 2 cloves garlic, minced
- 1 bay leaf
- Salt to taste
- 2-1/4 cups dry cannellini beans
- 28 oz. tomatoes
- 6 oz. tomato paste
- 2 cups chicken broth

Preparation:
1. Set the Ninja Foodi to sauté. Cook the bacon until crispy. Add the onion and garlic.
2. Cook for 2 minutes. Add the rest of the ingredients. Cover the pot. Set it to pressure.
3. Cook at high pressure for 40 minutes. Release the pressure naturally.
4. Season with salt and pepper.

Serving Suggestion: Top with the feta cheese.

Nutritional Information Per Serving:

Calories 367
Total Fat 6.7g
Saturated Fat 2g
Cholesterol 14mg
Sodium 626mg
Total Carbohydrate 54.4g
Dietary Fiber 20.3g
Total Sugars 9.5g
Protein 25.2g
Potassium 1742mg

8. Lemon Butter Green Beans

Serves: 4
Preparation time: 20 minutes

Ingredients:
- 1 lb. green beans
- 2 tablespoons olive oil
- 2 cloves garlic
- 1/4 cup lemon
- 1 tablespoon Parmesan cheese
- 2 tablespoons butter
- Salt and pepper to taste

Preparation:
1. Place the beans in a bowl. Coat with the oil. Season with the salt and pepper.
2. Put the green beans in the Ninja Foodi basket.
3. Cook at 390 degrees for 10 minutes, flipping halfway through.
4. Make the sauce by simmering the rest of the ingredients in the pot by pressing sauté.

Serving Suggestion: Serve as side dish to main course.

Tip: Add more Parmesan cheese if you like.

Nutritional Information Per Serving:

Calories 175
Total Fat 14.5g
Saturated Fat 5.7g

Cholesterol 20mg
Sodium 113mg
Total Carbohydrate 10.1g
Dietary Fiber 4.3g
Total Sugars 1.9g
Protein 4.6g
Potassium 263mg

Soups and Stews

1. Beef & Potato Stew

Categories:
Serves: 6
Preparation time: 1 hour and 15 minutes

Ingredients:

- 2 lb. boneless beef, sliced into cubes
- Salt and pepper to taste
- 3 tablespoons all-purpose flour
- 3 tablespoons olive oil
- 1 onion, chopped
- 1/2 teaspoon fresh rosemary leaves, chopped
- 1/2 teaspoon fresh thyme leaves, chopped
- 1/4 teaspoon dried oregano
- 1 tablespoon balsamic vinegar
- 2 cups beef broth
- 3 potatoes, sliced into cubes
- 1/2 teaspoon Worcestershire sauce

Preparation:

1. Season the beef with salt and pepper.
2. Coat with flour.
3. Pour the oil into the Ninja Foodi.
4. Press sauté.
5. Add the onion and cook for 1 minute.
6. Add the beef and cook until brown on both sides.
7. Add the rest of the ingredients.
8. Cover the pot.
9. Set it to pressure.
10. Cook at high pressure for 30 minutes.
11. Release pressure naturally.

Serving Suggestion: Garnish with chopped fresh parsley.
Tip: This can be stored in the refrigerator for up to 4 days.

Nutritional Information Per Serving:

Calories 433
Total Fat 16.5g
Saturated Fat 4.5g
Cholesterol 127mg
Sodium 360mg
Total Carbohydrate 22g
Dietary Fiber 3.2g
Total Sugars 2.3g
Protein 47.1g
Potassium 1109mg

2. Potato Soup

Categories:
Serves: 12
Preparation time: 1 hour and 15 minutes

Ingredients:

- 3 tablespoons butter
- 2 cloves garlic, minced
- 6 potatoes, diced
- 1/2 teaspoon pepper
- 2 teaspoons onion powder
- 1 cup chicken broth
- 1/4 teaspoon salt
- 2 cups milk
- 4 oz. cream cheese, softened
- 1 cup mozzarella cheese, shredded
- 1/2 cup bacon bits

Preparation:

1. Choose the sauté button in the Ninja Foodi.
2. Add the butter.
3. Wait for it to melt.
4. Cook the garlic for 2 minutes.
5. Add the potatoes and the rest of the ingredients except the milk, cheeses and bacon bits.
6. Seal the pot.
7. Choose pressure.
8. Cook at high pressure for 25 minutes.

9. Release the pressure naturally.
10. Take the potatoes out and mash with a fork.
11. Stir in the milk and cream cheese.
12. Put back the mashed potatoes.
13. Mix well.
14. Sprinkle the mozzarella and bacon bits on top.

Serving Suggestion: Serve with main course.

Tip: Use a potato masher to make things easier.

Nutritional Information Per Serving:

Calories 199
Total Fat 10.3g
Saturated Fat 5.6g
Cholesterol 30mg
Sodium 349mg
Total Carbohydrate 19.8g
Dietary Fiber 2.6g
Total Sugars 3.3g
Protein 7.4g
Potassium 529mg

3. Cauliflower Soup

Categories:
Serves: 4
Preparation time: 20 minutes

Ingredients:

- 2 tablespoons olive oil
- 1 onion, chopped
- 8 cups cauliflower florets
- 3 cups chicken stock
- 1 teaspoon garlic powder
- Salt to taste
- 4 oz. cream cheese, sliced into cubes
- 1 cup cheddar cheese, shredded
- 1/2 cup cream

Preparation:

1. Choose sauté in the Ninja Foodi.
2. Add the olive oil and cook onion for 2 minutes.

3. Add the rest of the ingredients except the cheeses and cream.
4. Set the pot to pressure.
5. Cover the pot.
6. Cook at high pressure for 5 minutes.
7. Release the pressure quickly.
8. Transfer the cauliflower in a food processor.
9. Pulse until smooth.
10. Put it back to the pot.
11. Stir in the cheeses and cream.
12. Serving Suggestion: Top with sour cream and crispy bacon bits.

Tip: Simmer to thicken the soup.

Nutritional Information Per Serving:

Calories 363
Total Fat 28.6g
Saturated Fat 14.4g
Cholesterol 67mg
Sodium 942mg
Total Carbohydrate 16.3g
Dietary Fiber 5.7g
Total Sugars 7.5g
Protein 14.3g
Potassium 737mg

4. Beef & Vegetable Soup

Categories:
Serves: 6
Preparation time: 1 hour and 10 minutes

Ingredients:

- 2 tablespoons olive oil
- 2 lb. stew beef
- 2 teaspoons all purpose seasoning
- 8 oz. tomato sauce
- 23 oz. tomato soup
- 1 tablespoon garlic powder
- 1 tablespoon onion powder
- Salt and pepper to taste
- 14 oz. green beans
- 14 oz. carrots, sliced

- 15 oz. sweet corn
- 1 cup potatoes, diced
- 1 cup water
- 2 cups beef broth

Preparation:

1. Hit the sauté button in the Ninja Foodi.
2. Add the oil and beef.
3. Sprinkle seasoning and toss to coat the beef evenly.
4. Cook until brown on all sides.
5. Drain the liquid.
6. In a bowl, mix the tomato sauce, tomato soup, garlic powder, onion powder, salt and pepper.
7. Pour this into the pot.
8. Add the rest of the ingredients.
9. Mix well.
10. Cover the pot.
11. Set it to pressure.
12. Cook at high pressure for 35 minutes.
13. Release the pressure naturally.

Nutritional Information Per Serving:

Calories 564
Total Fat 14.6g
Saturated Fat 1.3g
Cholesterol 0mg
Sodium 871mg
Total Carbohydrate 79.9g
Dietary Fiber 12.8g
Total Sugars 21.3g
Protein 39.1g
Potassium 1471mg

5. Ham & Potato Soup

Categories:
Serves: 4
Preparation time: 30 minutes

Ingredients:

- 2 tablespoons butter

- 1/2 cup carrots, sliced
- 1 onion, chopped
- 3 cloves garlic, minced
- 2 stalks celery, chopped
- 1 lb. cooked ham, cubed
- 2 lb. potatoes, cubed
- 32 oz. vegetable stock
- 1/4 cup coconut cream
- Salt and pepper to taste
- 1 teaspoon dried thyme

Preparation:

1. Select the sauté function in the Ninja Foodi.
2. Add the butter, onion, garlic, celery and carrot.
3. Cook for 5 minutes.
4. Add the rest of the ingredients except the cream.
5. Set it to pressure.
6. Cover the pot.
7. Cook at high pressure for 5 minutes.
8. Release the pressure quickly.
9. Stir in the cream before serving.

Serving Suggestion: Top with croutons.

Nutritional Information Per Serving:

Calories 434
Total Fat 15g
Saturated Fat 8g
Cholesterol 88mg
Sodium 532mg
Total Carbohydrates 51g
Dietary Fiber 4g
Sugars 6g
Protein 24g
Potassium 1430mg

6. Minestrone Soup

Categories:
Serves: 6
Preparation time: 30 minutes

Ingredients:

- 2 tablespoons olive oil
- 1 onion, diced
- 3 cloves garlic, minced
- 2 stalks celery, diced
- 2 carrots, peeled and diced
- 1 teaspoon dried oregano
- 1 1/2 teaspoons dried basil
- 1/2 teaspoon fennel seed
- 6 cups chicken broth
- 28 oz. diced tomatoes
- 16 oz. kidney beans, rinsed and drained
- 1 zucchini, chopped
- 1 bay leaf
- 1 cup kale, chopped
- 2 teaspoons red wine vinegar
- Salt and pepper to taste
- 1/4 cup Parmesan cheese, grated

Preparation:

1. Set the Ninja Foodi to sauté.
2. Add the oil.
3. Cook the onion, garlic, celery and carrots for 3 minutes.
4. Add the dried herbs and cook for 1 minute.
5. Add the rest of the ingredients except the kale and Parmesan.
6. Choose pressure.
7. Cover the pot.
8. Cook at high pressure for 5 minutes.
9. Release the pressure quickly.
10. Stir in the kale and wait for it to wilt and sprinkle Parmesan on top before serving.

Serving Suggestion: Garnish with chopped parsley.

Tip: Use low sodium chicken broth.

Nutritional Information Per Serving:

Calories 314
Total Fat 6.9g
Saturated Fat 1.9g
Cholesterol 5mg
Sodium 670mg

Total Carbohydrate 44.7g
Dietary Fiber 11.1g
Total Sugars 6.2g
Protein 20.5g
Potassium 1357mg

7. Tomato Basil Soup

Categories:
Serves: 8
Preparation time: 30 minutes

Ingredients:

- 1 tablespoon olive oil
- 1 cup onion, chopped
- 1 cup celery, chopped
- 1 cup carrot, chopped
- 30 oz. canned diced tomatoes, undrained
- 2 tablespoons tomato paste
- 4 cups chicken broth
- 1/4 cup fresh basil leaves, chopped
- 1 teaspoon dried oregano leaves
- 1/2 cup butter
- Salt and pepper to taste
- 1/2 cup all-purpose flour
- 1 cup Parmesan cheese, grated
- 1-1/2 cups half and half

Preparation:

1. Set the Ninja Foodi to sauté.
2. Pour in the oil.
3. Add the onion, celery and carrot.
4. Cook for 2 minutes.
5. Add the rest of the ingredients except the flour, Parmesan and half and half.
6. Seal the pot.
7. Set it to pressure. Cook at high pressure for 5 minutes.
8. Release the pressure naturally.
9. Pour the soup into a food processor. Pulse until smooth.
10. Pour it back to the pot.
11. Set it to sauté. Add the remaining ingredients.

12. Simmer for 5 minutes.

Serving Suggestion: Serve with toasted whole wheat bread.

Tip: Use freshly grated Parmesan cheese.

Nutritional Information Per Serving:

Calories 271
Total Fat 20.3g
Saturated Fat 11.5g
Cholesterol 50mg
Sodium 544mg
Total Carbohydrate 16.6g
Dietary Fiber 2.6g
Total Sugars 5.2g
Protein 7.3g
Potassium 570mg

8. Chicken & Lemon Soup

Categories:
Serves: 8
Preparation time: 30 minutes

Ingredients:

- 1 tablespoon olive oil
- 1 onion, diced
- 2 carrots, sliced
- 1 stalk celery, diced
- Salt and pepper to taste
- 2 chicken breasts, sliced into cubes
- 6 cups chicken broth
- 2 tablespoons butter
- 2 tablespoons flour dissolved in 2 tablespoons water
- 1/4 cup lemon juice

Preparation:

1. Set the Ninja Foodi to sauté.
2. Pour in the olive oil.
3. Add the onion and cook for 3 minutes.
4. Add the carrots, celery, salt and pepper.
5. Cook for 5 minutes.
6. Add the chicken and cook until brown on all sides.

7. Pour in the broth.
8. Seal the pot.
9. Set it to pressure.
10. Cook at high pressure for 5 minutes.
11. Release the pressure naturally.
12. Stir in the butter, flour and water mixture, and lemon juice.
13. Simmer for 5 minutes.

Serving Suggestion: Top with feta cheese cubes.

Tip: Use freshly squeezed lemon juice.

Nutritional Information Per Serving:

Calories 200
Total Fat 11.1g
Saturated Fat 4.2g
Cholesterol 52mg
Sodium 850mg
Total Carbohydrate 4.9g
Dietary Fiber 1g
Total Sugars 2.7g
Protein 18.9g
Potassium 433mg

Side Dishes

1. Garlic Mushrooms

Categories:
Serves: 2
Preparation time: 30 minutes

Ingredients:

- 1 lb. mushrooms, rinsed and drained
- 1 teaspoon onion powder
- Black pepper to taste
- 1 tablespoon minced garlic
- 2 teaspoons soy sauce

Preparation:

1. Mix all the ingredients in a bowl.
2. Put in the Ninja Foodi basket.
3. Seal the crisping lid.
4. Set it to air crisp.
5. Cook at 360 degrees F for 20 minutes.
6. Coat the beef cubes with the salt and pickling spice.
7. In a skillet over medium heat, pour in the olive oil.

Serving Suggestion: Sprinkle with chopped parsley.

Tip: Use low sodium soy sauce.

Nutritional Information Per Serving:

Calories 124
Total Fat 1.4g
Saturated Fat 0g
Cholesterol 0mg
Sodium 626mg
Total Carbohydrate 20.5g
Dietary Fiber 5g
Total Sugars 8.9g
Protein 15.7g
Potassium 1523mg

2. Mediterranean Vegetables

Categories:
Serves: 4
Preparation time: 30 minutes

Ingredients:

- 1 cup cherry tomatoes
- 1 eggplant, sliced into rounds
- 1 green bell pepper, sliced into strips
- 1 carrot, sliced into rounds
- 1 teaspoon mixed herbs
- 6 tablespoons olive oil
- 2 tablespoons honey
- 1 teaspoon mustard
- 2 teaspoons garlic puree
- Salt and pepper to taste

Preparation:

1. Drizzle the vegetables with the olive oil.
2. Add to the Ninja Foodi basket.
3. Seal the crisping lid.
4. Set it to air crisp.
5. Cook at 360 degrees F for 15 minutes.
6. Mix the rest of the ingredients.
7. Pour the sauce over the vegetables before serving.

Serving Suggestion: Garnish with lemon wedges.

Nutritional Information Per Serving:

Calories 269
Total Fat 21.6g
Saturated Fat 3g
Cholesterol 0mg
Sodium 16mg
Total Carbohydrate 21.3g
Dietary Fiber 5.6g
Total Sugars 15.6g
Protein 2.2g
Potassium 491mg

3. Fried Carrots, Zucchini and Squash

Categories:
Serves: 4
Preparation time: 50 minutes

Ingredients:

- 1/2 lb. carrots, cubed
- 6 teaspoons olive oil, divided
- 1 lb. zucchini, sliced into rounds
- 1 lb. squash, sliced into half moons
- Salt and pepper to taste
- 1 teaspoon dried tarragon

Preparation:

1. Toss the carrots in 2 teaspoons olive oil.
2. Place these in the Ninja Foodi basket.
3. Seal the crisping lid.
4. Choose air crisp function.
5. Cook at 400 degrees F for 5 minutes.
6. While waiting, drizzle the zucchini and squash in the remaining olive oil.
7. Season with the salt and pepper.
8. Add the zucchini and squash in the basket.
9. Cook at 400 degrees for 30 minutes.
10. Season with the tarragon.

Serving Suggestion: Garnish with chopped parsley.

Tip: Flip two to three times to cook evenly.

Nutritional Information Per Serving:

Calories 102
Total Fat 7.2g
Saturated Fat 1g
Cholesterol 0mg
Sodium 50mg
Total Carbohydrate 9.5g
Dietary Fiber 2.7g
Total Sugars 4.8g
Protein 1.9g
Potassium 483mg

4. Honey Roasted Carrots

Categories:
Serves: 4
Preparation time: 30 minutes

Ingredients:

- 3 cups carrots, sliced into chunks
- 1 tablespoon olive oil
- 1 tablespoon honey
- Salt and pepper to taste

Preparation:

1. Coat the carrots with the olive oil and honey.
2. Season with the salt and pepper.
3. Put in the Ninja Foodi basket.
4. Cover with the crisping lid.
5. Set it to air crisp.
6. Cook at 350 degrees F for 12 minutes.

Serving Suggestion: Sprinkle herbs on top.

Tip: Use organic honey

Nutritional Information Per Serving:

Calories 80
Total Fat 3.5g
Saturated Fat 0.5g
Cholesterol 0mg
Sodium 57mg
Total Carbohydrate 12.5g
Dietary Fiber 2.1g
Total Sugars 8.4g
Protein 0.7g
Potassium 267mg

5. Roasted Corn

Categories:
Serves: 4
Preparation time: 20 minutes

Ingredients:
- 4 ears of corn, husks removed and sliced into 2
- 2 teaspoons olive oil
- Salt and pepper to taste

Preparation:
1. Coat the corn with oil and season with salt and pepper.
2. Put in the Ninja Foodi basket.
3. Seal with the crisping lid.
4. Set it to air crisp.
5. Cook at 400 degrees F for 10 minutes.

Serving Suggestion: Sprinkle Parmesan cheese or brush with butter.

Tip: Use fresh ears of corn.

Nutritional Information Per Serving:
Calories 152
Total Fat 4.1g
Saturated Fat 0.6g
Cholesterol 0mg
Sodium 23mg
Total Carbohydrate 29g
Dietary Fiber 4.2g
Total Sugars 5g
Protein 5g
Potassium 416mg

6. Sweet Potato

Categories:
Serves: 3
Preparation time: 50 minutes

Ingredients:
3 sweet potatoes, washed and poked with fork
1 tablespoon olive oil
Salt and pepper to taste

Preparation:
1. Coat the sweet potato with olive oil.
2. Season with the salt and pepper.
3. Place in the Ninja Foodi basket.

4. Seal with the crisping lid.
5. Choose air crisp function.
6. Cook at 392 degrees F for 40 minutes.

Nutritional Information Per Serving:

Calories 109
Total Fat 2.5g
Saturated Fat 0.4g
Cholesterol 0mg
Sodium 7mg
Total Carbohydrate 20.9g
Dietary Fiber 3.1g
Total Sugars 0.4g
Protein 1.2g
Potassium 612mg

7. Lemon Parmesan Broccoli

Categories:
Serves: 4
Preparation time: 30 minutes

Ingredients:

- 6 cups water
- 2 lb. broccoli florets
- 2 tablespoons olive oil
- Salt and pepper to taste
- 1/4 cup Kalamata olives, pitted and sliced in half
- 2 teaspoons lemon zest, grated
- 1/4 cup Parmesan cheese, grated

Preparation:

1. Fill the Ninja Foodi with water.
2. Set it to sauté.
3. Let the water boil.
4. Add the broccoli and cook for 4 minutes.
5. Drain the water.
6. Toss the broccoli in olive oil and season with the salt and pepper.
7. Place in the basket and seal with the crisping lid.
8. Choose air crisp function.
9. Cook at 400 degrees F for 15 minutes.

10. Flip halfway through.
11. Toss the broccoli in the lemon zest and Parmesan cheese and mix with the olives.

Serving Suggestion: Serve with pasta or soup.

Tip: Use freshly grated Parmesan cheese.

Nutritional Information Per Serving:

Calories 170
Total Fat 10.2g
Saturated Fat 2.1g
Cholesterol 5mg
Sodium 224mg
Total Carbohydrate 16.1g
Dietary Fiber 6.2g
Total Sugars 3.9g
Protein 8.7g
Potassium 725mg

8. Garlic Mashed Potatoes

Categories:
Serves: 4
Preparation time: 30 minutes

Ingredients:

- 2 lb. potatoes, sliced into cubes
- 6 cloves garlic, crushed
- 2/3 cup chicken stock
- Salt and pepper to taste
- 3 tablespoons butter, divided
- 1/4 cup sour cream
- 1/4 cup cream cheese

Preparation:

1. Place the potatoes inside the Ninja Foodi.
2. Add the chicken stock, garlic, salt, pepper and 1/2 tablespoon butter.
3. Seal the pot.
4. Set it to pressure.
5. Cook at high pressure for 8 minutes.
6. Release the pressure naturally.

7. Mash the potatoes and stir in the rest of the ingredients and the remaining butter.

Serving Suggestion: Garnish with chopped chives.

Tip: Use sodium free chicken stock.

Nutritional Information Per Serving:

Calories 323
Total Fat 17.1g
Saturated Fat 10.6g
Cholesterol 45mg
Sodium 254mg
Total Carbohydrate 38.3g
Dietary Fiber 5.5g
Total Sugars 2.8g
Protein 5.8g
Potassium 984mg

Conclusion

As you can see, the Ninja Foodi is a versatile and multi-functional cooking device that lets you cook food in various ways.

That's not all. It also helps ensure that you create only the healthiest and delicious dishes for yourself and your family.

With this device, you can get started on a healthier lifestyle without putting too much burden and stress on yourself. You can whip up healthy dishes without having to spend too much time inside the kitchen.

Cheers to a healthier you!

Appendix 1: Measurement Conversion Table

Unit	Conversion	Conversion
1 teaspoon	1/3 tablespoon	1/6 ounce
1 tablespoon	3 teaspoons	1/2 ounce
1/8 cup	2 tablespoons	1 ounce
1/4 cup	4 tablespoons	2 ounces
1/3 cup	1/4 cup and 4 teaspoons	2-3/4 ounces
1/2 cup	8 tablespoons	4 ounces
1 cup	1/2 pint	8 ounces
1 pint	2 cups	16 ounces
1 quart	4 cups	32 ounces
1 liter	1 quart and 1/4 cup	4-1/4 cups
1 gallon	4 quarts	16 cups

Appendix 2: Common Healthy Food for Living

Apples
Avocados
Bananas
Blueberries
Oranges
Strawberries
Eggs
Lean Beef
Chicken Breasts
Lamb
Almonds
Chia Seeds
Coconuts
Macadamia Nuts
Walnuts
Peanuts
Asparagus
Bell Peppers
Broccoli
Carrots
Cauliflower
Cucumber
Garlic
Kale
Onions
Tomatoes
Fish and Seafood
Salmon
Shrimp
Tuna
Cod

Grains
Rice
Oats
Quinoa
Whole Wheat Bread
Green Beans
Kidney Beans
Lentils
Dairy Products
Soy Milk
Almond Milk
Cheese
Yogurt
Olive Oil
Grass Fed Butter
Coconut oil
Potatoes
Sweet Potatoes
Apple Cider Vinegar
Dark Chocolate